Guglielmo Gratarolo, Arthur Edward Waite

The Turba Philosophorum

Assembly of the Sages

Guglielmo Gratarolo, Arthur Edward Waite

The Turba Philosophorum
Assembly of the Sages

ISBN/EAN: 9783743393226

Manufactured in Europe, USA, Canada, Australia, Japa

Cover: Foto ©Thomas Meinert / pixelio.de

Manufactured and distributed by brebook publishing software (www.brebook.com)

Guglielmo Gratarolo, Arthur Edward Waite

The Turba Philosophorum

THE TURBA PHILOSOPHORUM.

PREFACE.

—:o:—

*T*HE *Turba Philosophorum* is indisputably the most ancient extant treatise on Alchemy in the Latin tongue, but it was not, so far as can be ascertained, originally written in Latin ; the compiler or editor, for in many respects it can scarcely be regarded as an original composition, wrote either in Hebrew or Arabic; however, the work, not only at the present day, but seemingly during the six or seven centuries when it was quoted as an authority by all the alchemical adepts, has been familiar only in its Latin garb. It is not, of course, certain that the original is irretrievably lost, the Arabic and Syriac manuscripts treating of early chemistry are preserved in considerable numbers in the various libraries of Europe, and have only been imperfectly explored. Unfortunately, the present editor has neither the opportunity nor the qualifications for undertaking such a task.

There are two codices or recensions of *The Turba Philosophorum*, which differ considerably from one another. What is called in the following pages the second recension, is appreciably shorter, clearer, and, on the whole, the less corrupt of the two, but they are both in a bad state. The longer recension has been chosen for the text of the following translation, because it seemed desirable to give the work in its entirety. The variations of the second recension are appended usually in foot-notes, but where the reading of the text is so corrupt as to be quite untranslatable, the editor has occasionally substituted that of the alternative version, and has in most cases indicated the course pursued.

Monsieur Berthelot's invaluable text and translation of the Byzantine Alchemists has been largely made use of, to illustrate the striking analogies between the Greek Hermetic writers of the fourth century and the Turba. It is to this great scholar and scientist that we owe the discovery of these analogies, some of which are very clearly indicated in a chapter devoted to the subject, and forming part of his " Essai sur la Transmission de la Science Antique au Moyen Age." It follows from M. Berthelot's researches, that Latin Alchemy, which has always been rightly referred to an Arabian source, connects with the Greek Alchemy which preceded Arabian Science, because the latter was itself derived from Greece. We are also enabled to identify, for the first time, and that with perfect certainty, those ancient sages, to whom all the Latin literature makes requent and reverent allusion ; we now know that they are Zosimus, the Panopolite, the adepts of the school of Democritus, and the other writers preserved in the Byzantine collection. M. Berthelot, however, infers that the Greek influence found in *The Turba Philosophorum* was not a direct influence, but was derived mediately through channels which are now unknown In any case the Turba summarises the author's preceding Geber, and is therefore the most valuable, as it is the most ancient, treatise on Alchemy, which exists in the Latin language.

The chief printed versions of *The Turba Philosophorum*, are those of the " Theatrum Chemicum," the "Bibliotheca Chemica Curiosa," and that of the smaller collection entitled " Artis Auriferæ Tractatus." There are some translations of the work existing in German and some also in French. Those in the latter language are specially remarkable for the very slender way in which they represent the original. The versions contained in Salmon's " Bibliothèque des Philosophes Alchimiques," and in the "Trois Anciens Traictés de la Philosophie Naturelle," are instances in point. One English version in manuscript is known to the present editor, and it will be found in the British Museum amongst the treasures of the Sloane collection. It is rendered, however, from the French, and has been found useless for the purposes of this translation.

It may be added that the great collections of Alchemy, such as the "Theatrum Chemicum" and Mangetus, contain colloquies, commentaries, and enigmas which pretend to elucidate the mysteries of *The Turba Philosophorum.* While they are of a considerably later date, they at the same time belong to the early period of Latin Alchemy. It may be added also that the editor has collected a considerable amount of material concerning this curious work, which the limits of the present volume preclude him from utilising.

ARTHUR EDWARD WAITE.

THE TURBA PHILOSOPHORUM,

TAKEN FROM AN ANCIENT MANUSCRIPT CODEX,
MORE PERFECT THAN ANY EDITION
PUBLISHED HERETOFORE.

———

The Epistle of Arisleus, prefixed to the Words of the Sages, concerning the purport of this Book, for the Benefit of Posterity, and the same being as here follows :—

ARISLEUS,* begotten of Pythagoras, a disciple of the disciples by the grace of thrice great Hermes, learning from the seat of knowledge, unto all who come after wisheth health and mercy. I testify that my

---

* An ancient gloss describes Arisleus as the son of Abladus. M. Berthelot supposes him to be synonymous with the Aristenes of the second recension (*Eleventh Dictum*) and of the *Exercitationes* on the *Turba*, which are found in the first volume of the *Bibliotheca Chemica*. Beyond the similarity of the name, and the fact that most names are mutilated in the *Turba*, there seems no reason to suppose that the compiler intended to connect Pythagoras with alchemical traditions through Aristeus, the sophist of the time of Antoninus.

master, Pythagoras,* the Italian, master of the wise and chief of the Prophets, had a greater gift of God and of Wisdom than was granted to any one after Hermes. Therefore he had a mind to assemble his disciples, who were now greatly increased, and had been constituted the chief persons throughout all regions for the discussion of this most precious Art, that their words might be a foundation for posterity. He then commanded Iximidrus, of highest council, to be the first speaker, who said :†—

---

* The Greek alchemists of the Byzantine Collection make no mention of Pythagoras, and the tradition which describes him as an adept of the Hermetic Mystery must be referred to an Arabian origin, to the treatises of El Habib, the Kitâb-al-Firhirst, and the true Geber, where alchemical writings attributed to this sage are freely quoted.

† The French version of Salmon has the following distinct variations :—" The beginning of the book, the Turba of the Philosophers, in which Arisleus has gathered together the sayings of the more prudent among the scholars, by introducing Pythagoras the Philosopher, that Master collecting the opinions of the scholars. The book is also called the Third Pythagorical Synod, instituted concerning

The First Dictum.

IXIMIDRUS *saith :*—I testify that the beginning of all things is a Certain Nature, which is perpetual, coequalling all things, and that the visible natures, with their births and decay, are times wherein the ends to which that nature brings them are beheld and summoned.* Now, I instruct you that the stars are igneous, and are kept within bounds by the air. If the humidity and density of the air did

Occult Philosophy. But Pythagoras commanded his scholar, Eximidrius, to begin the discourse," &c. The French translator seems to have summarised the recensions which he had collected, and to have put them, to some extent, in his own words. Here, however, he follows mainly the text of the second recension, the chief variation being that instead of " Occult Philosophy " the original reads " the vegetable stone."

* The same French Translation interprets this obscure passage as follows :—" The beginning of all things is a certain nature ; it is perpetual, infinite ; it nourishes and decocts all things. But this nature and the times of corruption and generation are, as it were, the terms by which it is attained unto, and which the universal nature nourishes and decocts." The second recension varies the last passage, as follows :—" The actions and passions thereof are known and understood only by those to whom a knowledge of the Sacred Art is given."

not exist to separate the flames of
the sun from living things, then the
Sun would consume all creatures.
But God has provided the separating
air, lest that which He has created
should be burnt up. Do you not
observe that the Sun when it rises in
the heaven overcomes the air by its
heat, and that the warmth penetrates
from the upper to the lower parts of
the air? If, then, the air did not
presently breathe forth those winds
whereby creatures are generated, the
Sun by its heat would certainly destroy
all that lives. But the Sun is kept
in check by the air, which thus conquers because it unites the heat of the
Sun to its own heat, and the humidity
of water to its own humidity. Have
you not remarked how tenuous water
is drawn up into the air by the action
of the heat of the Sun, which thus
helps the water against itself? If the
water did not nourish the air by such
tenuous moisture, assuredly the Sun
would overcome the air. The fire,

therefore, extracts moisture from the water, by means of which the air conquers the fire itself. Thus, fire and water are enemies between which there is no consanguinity, for the fire is hot and dry, but the water is cold and moist. The air, which is warm and moist, joins these together by its concording medium ; between the humidity of water and the heat of fire the air is thus placed to establish peace. And look ye all how there shall arise a spirit from the tenuous vapour of the air, because the heat being joined to the humour, there necessarily issues something tenuous, which will become a wind. For the heat of the Sun extracts something tenuous out of the air, which also becomes spirit and life to all creatures. All this, however, is disposed in such manner by the will of God, and a coruscation appears when the heat of the Sun touches and breaks up a cloud.

The TURBA *saith :*—Well hast thou described the fire, even as thou knowest concerning it, and thou hast believed the word of thy brother.

The Second Dictum.

EXUMDRUS *saith :*—I do magnify the air according to the mighty speech of Iximidrus, for the work is improved thereby. The air is inspissated, and it is also made thin ; it grows warm and becomes cold. The inspissation thereof takes place when it is divided in heaven by the elongation of the Sun ; its rarefaction is when, by the exaltation of the Sun in heaven, the air becomes warm and is rarefied. It is comparable with the complexion of Spring,* in the distinction of time, which is neither warm nor cold. For according to the mutation of the con-

---

* A similar comparison is used in the Arabian *Book of Crates*, where it is enjoined that the operation of the philosophical fire upon the philosophical matter should be regulated after the same manner as Nature regulates the influence of the four seasons ; and the same treatise, moreover, represents still older expositions of alchemical philosophy as using the same illustration. It is probable that the *Turba* in its original form antedated the *Book of Crates*.

stituted disposition with the altering distinctions of the soul, so is Winter altered. The air, therefore, is inspissated when the Sun is removed from it, and then cold supervenes upon men.

Whereat the TURBA *said :*—Excellently hast thou described the air, and given account of what thou knowest to be therein.

The Third Dictum.

ANAXAGORAS *saith :*—I make known that the beginning of all those things which God hath created is weight and proportion,* for weight rules all things, and the weight and spissitude of the earth is manifest in proportion ; but weight is not found except in body. And know, all ye Turba, that the spissitude of the four elements reposes in the earth ; for the spissitude of

---

* The original is *pietas et ratio,* but the technical use of the term *pietas* by the Hebrew or Arabic original seems obviously to connect it with the sense of the Hebrew *Paz,* signifying compactness. Compare also the Greek verb *Piezo,* to press or squeeze down.

fire falls into air, the spissitude of air, together with the spissitude received from the fire, falls into water; the spissitude also of water, increased by the spissitude of fire and air, reposes in earth. Have you not observed how the spissitude of the four elements is conjoined in earth? The same, therefore, is more inspissated than all. *Then saith the* TURBA: —Thou hast well spoken. Verily the earth is more inspissated than are the rest. Which, therefore, is the most rare of the four elements and is most worthy to possess the rarity of these four? *He answereth* :—Fire is the most rare among all, and thereunto cometh what is rare of these four. But air is less rare than fire, because it is warm and moist, while fire is warm and dry; now that which is warm and dry is more rare than the warm and moist. *They say unto him:* —Which element is of less rarity than air? *He answereth* :—Water, since cold and moisture inhere therein, and every cold humid is of less rarity than a warm humid. *Then do they say unto him :*—Thou hast spoken truly. What, therefore, is of less rarity than water ? *He answereth :*—Earth, because it is cold and dry, and that which is cold and dry is of less rarity than that which is cold and moist. PYTHAGORAS *saith :*—Well have ye provided, O Sons of the Doctrine, the description of these four natures,* out of which God hath created all things. Blessed, therefore, is he who comprehends what ye have declared, for from the apex of the world he shall not find an intention greater than his own ! Let us, therefore, make perfect our discourse. *They reply :*—Direct every one to take up our speech in turn. Speak thou, O Pandolfus !

---

* "You have been told . . . that the ancients discoursed of four elements. Know that it is by means of these four elements that humid and dry things are constituted, as also things warm and cold, the male and the female. Two [elements] rise up and two fall down. The two ascending elements are fire and air ; the two descending elements are earth and water."—Olympiodorus *On the Sacred Art.*

The Fourth Dictum.

But PANDOLFUS *saith :*—I signify to posterity that air is a tenuous matter of water, and that it is not separated from it. It remains above the dry earth, to wit, the air hidden in the water, which is under the earth. If this air did not exist, the earth would not remain above the humid water. *They answer :*—Thou hast said well ; complete, therefore, thy speech. *But he continueth : —* The air which is hidden in the water under the earth is that which sustains the earth, lest it should be plunged into the said water ; and it, moreover, prevents the earth from being overflowed by that water. The province of the air is, therefore, to fill up and to make separation between diverse things, that is to say, water and earth, and it is constituted a peacemaker between hostile things, namely, water and fire, dividing these, lest they destroy one another. *The* TURBA *saith :*—If you gave an illustration hereof, it would be clearer to those who do not understand. *He answereth :*—An egg is an illustration, for therein four things are conjoined; the visible cortex or shell represents the earth, and the albumen, or white part, is the water.* But a very thin inner cortex is joined to the outer cortex, representing, as I have signified to you, the separating medium between earth and water, namely, that air which divides the earth from the water. The yolk also of the egg represents fire; the cortex which contains the yolk corresponds to that

---

* The allegory of the philosophical egg can be traced to the Greek alchemists. A short treatise is still extant under this title, and another on the *Nomenclature of the Egg*, which is described as the Mystery of the Art. It is composed of four elements, because it is the image of the world. It is the stone which is not a stone, the stone of copper, the Armenian stone, &c. The shell is likened to the earth, being cold and dry; it has been named copper, iron, tin, lead. The white of the egg is divine water, water of the sea, water of alum, &c. The yolk is copperas, native sulphur, mercury, &c. The oily part (? the chicken) is fire. But the egg, symbolical, as it is, is sometimes itself described symbolically, after the similitude of a seed; the shell is likened to the skin which covers the seed; the white and the yolk are the flesh, and the watery part is the breath, or air.

other air which separates the water from the fire. But they are both one and the same air, namely, that which separates things frigid, the earth from the water, and that which separates the water from the fire. But the lower air is thicker than the upper air, and the upper air is more rare and subtle, being nearer to the fire than the lower air. In the egg, therefore, are four things—earth, water, air, and fire. But the point of the Sun, these four excepted, is in the centre of the yolk, and this is the chicken. Consequently, all philosophers in this most excellent art have described the egg as an example, which same thing they have set over their work.

The Fifth Dictum.

ARISLEUS *saith :*—Know that the earth is a hill and not a plain, for which reason the Sun does not ascend over all the zones of the earth in a single hour; but if it were flat, the sun would rise in a moment over the whole earth.

PARMENIDES *saith :*—Thou hast spoken briefly, O Arisleus ! *He answereth :*—Is there anything the Master has left us which bears witness otherwise ? Yet I testify that God is one, having never engendered or been begotten, and that the head of all things after Him is earth and fire, because fire is tenuous and light, and it rules all things on earth, but the earth, being ponderous and gross, sustains all things which are ruled by fire.

The Sixth Dictum.

LUCAS *saith :*—You speak only about four natures ; and each one of you observes something concerning these. Now, I testify unto you that all things which God hath created are from these four natures, and the things which have been created out of them return into them. In these living creatures are generated and die, and all things take place as God hath predestinated. DEMOCRITUS, *the disciple of* LUCAS, *answereth :*—Thou hast well spoken, O

Lucas, when dealing with the four natures ! *Then saith* ARISLEUS :—O Democritus, since thy knowledge was derived from Lucas, it is presumption to speak among those who are well acquainted with thy master ! LUCAS *answereth:*—Albeit Democritus received from me the science of natural things, that knowledge was derived from the philosophers of the Indies and from the Babylonians ; I think he surpasses those of his own age in this learning. *The* TURBA *answereth :*—When he attains to that age* he will give no small satisfaction, but being in his youth he should keep silence.

The Seventh Dictum.

LOCUSTA *saith :*—All those creatures which have been described by Lucas are two only, of which one is neither

---

* Whether the age indicated is that of the Indian and Babylonian adepts does not appear, but the entire episode is remarkable when it is borne in mind what great importance evidently attached to the Democritic school of Greek alchemy. It seems to indicate that the TURBA PHILO-SOPHORUM represents a tradition hostile to the tradition of

known nor expressed, except by piety, for it is not seen or felt. PYTHAGORAS *saith* :—Thou hast entered upon a subject which, if completed, thou wilt describe subtly. State, therefore, what is this thing which is neither felt, seen, nor known. *Then he* :—It is that which is not known, because in this world it is discerned by reason without the clients thereof, which are sight, hearing, taste, smell, and touch. O Crowd of the Philosophers, know you not that it is only sight which can distinguish white from black, and hearing only which can discriminate between a good and bad word! Similarly, a wholesome odour cannot be separated by reason from one which is fetid, except through the sense of smell, nor can sweetness be discriminated from bitterness save by means of taste, nor smooth from rough unless

---

Democritus, who, accordingly, figures merely as a promising tyro, and, in fact, remains silent throughout the rest of the deliberations. For "those of his own age" the second recension reads "his contemporaries."

by touch.   *The* TURBA *answereth :—*
Thou hast well spoken, yet hast thou
omitted to treat of that particular
thing which is not known, or described,
except by reason and piety.   *Saith he :*
—Are ye then in such haste?   Know
that the creature which is cognised in
none of these five ways is a sublime
creature, and, as such, is neither seen
nor felt, but is perceived by reason
alone, of which reason Nature con-
fesses that God is a partaker.   *They
answer :*—Thou   hast   spoken   truly
and excellently.   *And he :*—I will now
give a further explanation.   Know that
this creature, that is to say, the world,
hath a light, which is the Sun, and the
same is more subtle than all other
natures, which light is so ordered that
living beings may attain to vision.
But if this subtle light were removed,
they would become darkened, seeing
nothing, except the light of the moon,
or of the stars, or of fire, all which are
derived from the light of the Sun,
which causes all creatures to give light.

For this God has appointed the Sun to be the light of the world, by reason of the attenuated nature of the Sun. And know that the sublime creature before mentioned has no need of the light of this Sun, because the Sun is beneath that creature, which is more subtle and more lucid. This light, which is more lucid than the light of the Sun, they have taken from the light of God, which is more subtle than their light. Know also that the created world is composed of two dense things and two rare things, but nothing of the dense is in the sublime creature. Consequently the Sun is rarer than all inferior creatures. *The* TURBA *answereth* :—Thou hast excellently described what thou hast related. And if, good Master, thou shalt utter anything whereby our hearts may be vivified, which now are mortified by folly, thou wilt confer upon us a great boon !*

---

* The shortened version of the second Recension offers some conspicuous variations, and is literally as

The Eighth Dictum.

PYTHAGORAS *saith* :—I affirm that God existed before all things, and with Him was nothing, as He was at first. But know, all ye Philosophers, that I declare this in order that I may fortify your opinion concerning these four elements and arcana, as well as in the sciences thereof, at which no one can arrive save by the will of God. Understand, that when God was alone, He created four things—fire, air, water, and earth, out of which things He afterwards

---

follows :—" Two natures alone are described by Lucas, one of which is neither known nor realised, save by piety and reason ; the other is not seen and is not described, for it is heaven. But there is a third connected nature, which is felt, seen, and known, and this is that which contains whatsoever is in heaven or earth. Now, reason perceives by the help of the five senses, &c. . . . What ensues is substantially the same as the text, till towards the close, which is as follows :—As to that nature which is perceived by none of these, the same is sublime ; it is known by reason and piety only, and is God Most High, who made the light which is the Sun. Know that the Sun is more subtle than all creatures, to the end that it may light the world, which consists of two dense things and two rare. Nothing of the dense is in the sublime creation, because He himself is more rare than the Sun and all inferior creatures."

created all others, both the sublime and the inferior, because He predestinated from the beginning that all creatures extracted from water should multiply and increase, that they might dwell in the world and perform His judgments therein. Consequently, before all, He created the four elements, out of which He afterwards created what He willed, that is to say, diverse creatures, some of which were produced from a single element.* *The* Turba *saith*:—Which are these, O Master ? *And he*:—They are the angels, whom He created out of fire. *But the* Turba :—Which, then, are created out of two ? *And he*:—Out of the elements of fire and air are the

---

* In the *Book of Balances*, one of the genuine Arabian works of Geber, there is a passage which has some analogy with this *dictum*:—"After God had created all things of the four elements . . . He caused the four qualities to issue from the ancient worlds : namely, heat, cold, moisture, and dryness. The combination of these elements produced fire, which contains heat and dryness ; water, which possesses cold and moisture ; air, which has warmth and humidity ; earth, which is cold and dry. By the help of these elements God created the superior and inferior worlds."

sun, moon, and stars composed.
Hence the angels are more lucid than
the sun, moon, and stars, because they
are created from one substance, which
is less dense than two, while the sun
and the stars are created from a composition of fire and air. *The* TURBA
saith : — And what concerning the
creation of Heaven ? *Then he* :—God
created the Heaven out of water and
air, whence this is also composed of
two, namely, the second of the rarer
things, which is air, and the second
of the denser things, which is water.
And they :—Master, continue thy discourse concerning these three, and rejoice our hearts with thy sayings,
which are life to the dead. *But the
other answereth* :—I notify to you that
God hath further made creatures out
of three and out of four ; out of three
are created flying things, beasts, and
vegetables ; some of these are created
out of water, air, and earth, some out
of fire, air, and earth. *But the* TURBA
saith :—Distinguish these divers crea-

tures one from another. *And he*:—
Beasts are created out of fire, air, and
earth; flying things out of fire, air,
and water, because flying things, and
all among vegetables which have a
spirit, are created out of water, while
all brute animals are from earth, air,
and fire. Yet in vegetables there is no
fire, for they are created out of earth,
water, and air. *Whereat the* TURBA
saith:—Let us assume that a fire, with
your reverence's pardon, does reside in
vegetables. *And he*:—Ye have spoken
the truth, and I affirm that they contain fire. *And they*:—Whence is that
fire? *He answereth*:—Out of the heat
of the air which is concealed therein;
for I have signified that a thin fire is
present in the air, but the elementary
fire concerning which you were in doubt
is not produced, except in things which
have spirit and soul. But out of four
elements our father Adam and his sons
were created,* that is, of fire, air,

---

* The treatise of Olympiodorus *On the Sacred Art*
observes that Adam was the issue of the four elements, and

water, and likewise earth. Understand, all ye that are wise, how everything which God hath created out of
one essence dies not until the Day of
Judgment. The definition of death
is the disjunction of the composite, but
there is no disjunction of that which is
simple, for it is one. Death consists
in the separation of the soul from the
body, because anything formed out of
two, three, or four components must
disintegrate, and this is death. Understand, further, that no complex
substance which lacks fire eats, drinks,
or sleeps, because in all things which
have a spirit fire is that which eats.*

---

terms him virgin earth, igneous earth, carnal earth, and
sanguineous earth, making reference to the libraries of
Ptolemy. There are similar references in Zosimus, by
whom he is identified with death. But the carnal Adam
of Zosimus signifies material humanity in general, and
therein is contained the spiritual man, whose name no one
knoweth except Nicotheos, and that mysterious personage,
the alchemist himself acknowledges to be undiscoverable.
The substitute for his true name signifies light and fire.

* The nature of the angels, and the question whether
they eat and sleep, does not seem to have been discussed
either by Greek, Syriac, or Arabian alchemists. Zosimus
narrates that the art of alchemy was revealed to mortals by

The TURBA *answereth* :—How is it, Master, that the angels, being created of fire, do not eat, seeing thou assertest that fire is that which eats! *And he* : Hence ye doubt, each having his opinion, and ye are become opponents, but if ye truly knew the elements, ye would not deny these things. I agree with all whose judgment it is that simple fire eats not, but thick fire. The angels, therefore, are not created out of thick fire, but out of the thinnest of very thin fire ; being created, then, of that which is most simple and exceedingly thin, they neither eat, drink, nor sleep. *And the* TURBA :— Master, our faculties are able to perceive, for by God's assistance we have

---

the fallen angels ; it is to them that the tradition of the art must be referred as to a primary source ; and it was they also who wrote the primeval books of alchemy. It will be remembered that magic was also one of the mysteries unfolded by the same intelligences. In the discourse of Isis to Horus, the Mother of the Gods appears as a prophetess who obtained initiation into the mysteries of alchemy from the great angel Amnaël, who desired to possess her.

exhausted thy sayings, but our faculties
of hearing and of sight are unable to
carry such great things. May God
reward thee for the sake of thy disciples, since it is with the object of
instructing future generations that thou
hast summoned us together from our
countries, the recompense of which
thou wilt not fail to receive from the
Judge to come ! ARISLEUS *saith* :—
Seeing that thou hast gathered us
together for the advantage of posterity,
I think that no explanations will be
more useful than definitions of those
four elements which thou hast taught
us to attain. *And he* :—None of you
are, I suppose, ignorant that all the
Wise have propounded definitions in
God. *The* TURBA *answereth* :—Should
your disciples pass over anything, it
becomes you, O Master, to avoid
omissions for the sake of future generations. *And he:*—If it please you, I
will begin the disposition here, since
envious men in their books have
separated that, or otherwise I will put

it at the end of the book.* *Whereat the*
TURBA *saith*:—Place it where you
think it will be clearest for future
generations. *And he*:—I will place it
where it will not be recognised by the
foolish,† nor ignored by the Sons of the
Doctrine, for it is the key, the perfection
and the end.

The Ninth Dictum.

EXIMENUS *saith*:—God hath created all
things by his word, having said unto
them: Be, and they were made, with the
four other elements, earth, water, air,
and fire, which He coagulated, and
things contrary were commingled, for
we see that fire is hostile to water, water

---

* The necessity of concealing the Art is one of the
chief anxieties of the Greek alchemists. Isis herself is
sworn to secrecy by heaven and earth and hell, by the four
elements, by the height and the depth, by Hermes, by
Anubis, and by the howlings of Kerkoros. "An oath has
been required of us to reveal nothing clearly to any [un-
initiated] person," says Democritus in the *Epistle of
Synesius to Dioscorus.*

† The reader will not fail to observe the artless way in
which this passage betrays the whole dialogue as a literary
composition.

hostile to fire, and both are hostile to
earth and air. Yet God hath united
them peacefully, so that they love one
another. Out of these four elements,
therefore, are all things created—heaven
and the throne thereof; the angels; the
sun, moon, and stars; earth and sea,
with all things that are in the sea, which
indeed are various, and not alike, for
their natures have been made diverse by
God, and also the creations. But the
diversity is more than I have stated;
each of these natures is of diverse nature, and by a legion of diversities is the
nature of each diverse. Now this diversity subsists in all creatures, because
they were created out of diverse elements. Had they been created out of
one element, they would have been
agreeing natures. But diverse elements
being here mingled, they lose their own
natures, because the dry being mixed
with the humid and the cold combined
with the hot, become neither cold nor
hot; so also the humid being mixed
with the dry becomes neither dry nor

humid. But when the four elements are commingled, they agree, and thence proceed creatures which never attain to perfection, except they be left by night to putrefy and become visibly corrupt. God further completed his creation by means of increase, food, life, and government. Sons of the Doctrine, not without purpose have I described to you the disposition of these four elements, for in them is a secret arcanum ; two of them are perceptible to the sense of touch and vision, and of these the operation and virtue are well known. These are earth and water. But there are two other elements which are neither visible nor tangible, which yield naught, whereof the place is never seen, nor are their operations and force known, save in the former elements, namely, earth and water ; now when the four elements are not commingled, no desire of men is accomplished. But being mixed, departing from their own natures, they become another thing. Over these let us meditate very carefully. *And the*

TURBA :—Master, if you speak, we will give heed to your words. *Then he* :—I have now discoursed, and that well. I will speak only useful words which ye will follow as spoken. Know, all present, that no true tincture is made except from our copper.* Do not therefore, exhaust your brains and your money, lest ye fill your hearts with sorrow. I will give you a fundamental axiom, that unless you turn the aforesaid copper† into

---

* At this point there appears to be a sudden transition from cosmology to alchemy, but it must be remembered that it is one of the Hermetic Methods to describe the processes of the great work in the language of cosmology, and this not only in the Latin mediæval writers, but also in the Greek. For example, the Byzantine fragment entitled *The Nomenclature of the Egg* affirms that the egg is the image of the world, and hence is composed of the four elements.

† The philosophical copper is a subject of continual reference throughout all alchemy. Among the earliest authorities, the *Book of Crates* says that copper, like man, has a spirit, soul, and body. It appears from the same treatise that the term is symbolical, and applies to a stage of the alchemical process. Another passage describes it as the essential substance. Gold is said to transform only with lead and copper. The *Lexicon of Chrysopeia* explains that white copper is crude sulphur.

white, and make visible coins* and then afterwards again turn it into redness,† until a Tincture‡ results, verily, ye accomplish nothing. Burn therefore the copper, break it up, deprive it of its blackness by cooking, imbuing, and washing, until the same becomes white. Then rule it.

---

* M. Berthelot has pointed out that the use of the term *nummus* by the Latin alchemists is a misconception of the meaning of anterior writers. The reference is to *Asem*, an alloy of gold and silver.

† Numerous preparations for whitening and reddening will be found in the Collection of Ancient Greek Alchemists, as, for example, the *Combination of the White Preparation* in the Address of *Isis to Horus*, the recipe in the twenty-first paragraph of the *Natural Questions* of Democritus, again in the *Book of Synesius, the Philosopher, addressed to Dioscorus*, and elsewhere in many places. It is invariably an operation with copper. The book addressed by Democritus to Leucippus says that the alchemical work comprises the process of making white and making yellow (red), as also the softening and coction of the mineral of copper. According to Synesius, the process of whitening is a calcination, and making yellow is an igneous regeneration.

‡ The Greek Lexicon of Chrysopeia distinguishes two species of tincture, that which so permeates and soaks into a substance as to change its nature, and that which produces a superficial colouring.

The Tenth Dictum.

ARISLEUS *saith* :—Know that the key of this work is the art of Coins.* Take, therefore, the body which I have shewn to you and reduce it to thin tablets. Next immerse the said tablets in the Water of our Sea,† which is permanent Water,‡ and, after it is covered,§ set it over a gentle fire until the tablets are melted and become waters or Etheliæ,

---

* In this instance the term appears to be used as the equivalent of tablets or *lamina*—the thin strips into which later alchemy frequently directs a metal to be cut before it is subjected to a given treatment.

† Pelagus, cited by Olympiodorus in the *Treatise on the Sacred Art*, quotes Zosimus in definition of the sea as the hermaphrodytic element.

‡ The Book of *El-Habib* says that the virtue of eternal water is that of a spiritual blood. It is identified with æriform water, azure water, and water of sulphur. It is also primal sulphur. When boiled, it transforms the male (arsenic) into silver, and afterwards into gold. It is also said that copper is water of silver, which, after preparation, becomes eternal water. Interpreting later writers, Rulandus says that it is the philosophical solution of two perfect bodies, and he enumerates the contradictory names which have been assigned to it in alchemy.

§ The reference is apparently to the closing of the mouth of the vessel.

which are one and the same thing.
Mix, cook, and simmer in a gentle fire
until Brodium is produced, like to
Saginatum. Then stir in its water of
Etheliæ until it be coagulated, and the
coins become variegated, which we call
the Flower of Salt. Cook it, therefore,
until it be deprived of blackness, and
the whiteness appear. Then rub it, mix
with the Gum of Gold, and cook until
it becomes red Etheliæ. Use patience
in pounding lest you become weary.
Imbue the Ethelia with its own water,
which has preceded from it, which also
is Permanent Water, until the same
becomes red. This, then, is Burnt
Copper,* which is the Leaven of Gold
and the Flower thereof. Cook the
same with Permanent Water, which is

---

* A short excursus *On the Diversity of Burnt Copper*
is preserved among the writings of Zosimus, where it is
noted that many persons prepare it by means of sulphur,
and a process with sulphurated iron is quoted with high
approbation from Democritus. Burnt copper is elsewhere
defined by the same author as " the metal rendered blood-
colour (in view of whitening) and tinged within and
without."

always with it, until the water be dried
up. Continue the operation until all
the water is consumed, and it becomes
a most subtle powder.

The Eleventh Dictum.

PARMENIDES *saith* :—Ye must know
that envious men have dealt volu-
minously with several waters, brodiums,
stones, and metals, seeking to deceive
all you who aspire after knowledge.
Leave, therefore, all these, and make
the white red, out of this our copper,
taking copper and lead, letting these
stand for the grease, or blackness, and
tin for the liquefaction. Know ye,
further, that unless ye rule the Nature
of Truth, and harmonize well together
its complexions and compositions, the
consanguineous with the consanguineous, and the first with the first, ye
act improperly and effect nothing,
because natures will meet their natures,
follow them, and rejoice. For in them
they putrefy and are generated, because
Nature is ruled by Nature, which

destroys it, turns it into dust, reduces to nothing, and finally herself renews it, repeats, and frequently produces the same. Therefore look in books, that ye may know the Nature of Truth, what putrefies it and what renews, what savour it possesses, what neighbours it naturally has, and how they love each other, how also after love enmity and corruption intervene, and how these natures should be united one to another and made at peace, until they become gentle in the fire in similar fashion. Having, therefore, noticed the facts in this Art, set your hands to the work. If indeed, ye know not the Natures of Truth, do not approach the work, since there will follow nothing but harm, disaster, and sadness. Consider, therefore, the teaching of the Wise, how they have declared the whole work in this saying :—Nature rejoices in Nature, and Nature contains Nature. In these words there is shewn forth unto you the whole work. Leave, therefore, manifold and superfluous things, and take

quicksilver,* coagulate in the body of
Magnesia,† in Kuhul, or in Sulphur
which does not burn ; make the same
nature white, and place it upon our
Copper, when it becomes white. And
if ye cook still more, it becomes red,
when if ye proceed to coction, it becomes
gold. I tell you that it turns the sea
itself into red and the colour of gold.
Know ye also that gold is not turned
into redness save by Permanent Water,
because Nature rejoices in Nature.‡

---

* Mercury, according to the Greek Epistle of Synesius,
is like wax, which readily assumes any colour that is
imparted to it, for Mercury whitens all bodies and attracts
their souls ; it digests them by coction, and takes complete
possession of them.

† The Magnesia of Alchemy is not common Magnesia,
and this remark applies equally to the Greek Alchemists,
who are the inspiration of the *Turba Philosophorum*, to
that treatise, and to the later adepts. In one of the
treatises belonging to the school of Democritus the sign of
Cinnabar follows the term. The body of Magnesia is
mentioned in the discourse of Synesius and Dioscorus ; and
on the Metallic Body of Magnesia, Zosimus has a special
treatise with reference to the method by which it is
whitened. According to Synesius it signifies the mixture
of substances.

‡ The formulæ which are so frequently repeated in the
Turba Philosophorum : Nature rejoices in Nature : Nature

Reduce, therefore, the same by means of cooking into a humour, until the hidden nature appear. If, therefore, it be manifested externally, seven times imbue the same with water, cooking, imbuing, and washing, until it become red. O those celestial natures, multiplying the natures of truth by the will of God! O that potent Nature, which overcame and conquered natures, and caused its natures to rejoice and be glad!* This, therefore, is that special and spiritual nature to which the God thereof can give what fire cannot. Consequently, we glorify and magnify that [species], than which nothing is more precious in the true tincture, or the like in the smallest degree to be found. This is that truth

---

overcomes nature: Nature contains Nature: Nature is ruled by Nature: are derived literally from the Greek Alchemists.

* These alchemical Grand Antiphons in O are either literally borrowed from the Greek alchemists, or are formed on the model of precisely similar exclamations in those writers:—" O, Supreme Wonder ! O, most happy and Sovereign Matter," &c.

which those investigating wisdom love.
For when it is liquefied with bodies, the
highest operation is effected. If ye
knew the truth, what great thanks ye
would give me ! Learn, therefore, that
while you are tingeing the cinders, you
must destroy those that are mixed.
For it overcomes those which are mixed,
and changes them to its own colour. And
as it visibly overcame the surface, even
so it mastered the interior. And if
one be volatile but the other endure
the fire, either joined to the other
endures the fire. Know also, that
if the vapours have whitened the
surfaces, they will certainly whiten the
interiors. Know further, all ye seekers
after Wisdom, that one matter overcomes four, and our Sulphur* alone
consumes all things. *The Turba
answereth* : Thou hast spoken excellently

---

* Sulphur, Mercury, and Salt figure in all Hermetic literature as the most indispensable principles of the *Magnum
Opus*. The later writers never weary of affirming that they
are not the substances commonly so called, but this does
not appear so plainly in earlier and especially in Greek
Authors.

well, O Parmenides, but thou hast not demonstrated the disposition of the smoke to posterity, nor how the same is whitened !

The Twelfth Dictum.

LUCAS *saith :* I will speak at this time, following the steps of the ancients. Know, therefore, all ye seekers after Wisdom, that this treatise is not from the beginning of the ruling !* Take quicksilver,† which is from the male, and coagulate according to custom. Observe that I am speaking to you in accordance with custom, because it has been already coagulated. Here, therefore, is not the beginning of the ruling, but I prescribe this method,

---

* A further insight into the artificial character of the book is afforded at this point. The meaning which is designed to be conveyed is, that in common with many other alchemical works, the instruction begins in the middle of the process—for the more complete confusion of the uninitiated.

† It should be noted in this connection that the attribution of the seven metals to the seven planets is not found in the *Turba*. Thus, quicksilver is never spoken of as Mercury, nor gold as Sol, &c.

namely, that you shall take the quicksilver from the male, and shall either
impose upon iron, tin, or governed
copper, and it will be whitened.*

White Magnesia is made in the same
way, and the male is converted with
it. But forasmuch as there is a
certain affinity between the magnet
and the iron, therefore our nature
rejoices.† Take, then, the vapour
which the Ancients commanded you
to take, and cook the same with its
own body until tin is produced. Wash
away its blackness according to custom,
and cleanse and roast at an equable
fire until it be whitened. But every body
is whitened with governed quicksilver,
for Nature converts Nature. Take, therefore, Magnesia, Water of Alum, Water
of Nitre, Water of the Sea, and Water
of Iron ; whiten with smoke.‡ What-

---

* The second recension reads : " Ye shall impose
upon copper, that is, governed iron, and it shall be
whitened."

† The alternative reading is : " Therefore Nature also
rejoices in Nature."

‡ Hermes, as quoted by Olympiodorus, defines smoke
as intermediary between the warm and the dry.

soever ye desire to be whitened is whitened with this smoke, because it is itself white, and whitens all things. Mix, therefore, the said smoke with its fæces until it be coagulated and become excessively white.* Roast this white copper till it germinates of itself, since the Magnesia when whitened does not suffer the spirits to escape, or the shadow of copper† to appear, because Nature contains Nature. Take, therefore, all ye Sons of the Doctrine, the white sulphureous nature, whiten with salt and dew, or with the Flower of White Salt,‡ until it become

---

* The alternative reading is : "until it shall become a white coin or tablet."

† The shadow of copper is the flower of copper, *i.e.*, M. Berthelot explains, protoxide, verdegris. The epistle of Democritus to Leucippus explains that a metal without shadow is a brilliant metal. Zosimus says that the act of burning is called the destruction of the shadow. Pelagus defines the shadow of copper as the black tinge which it produces in silver. Democritus also gives a recipe for the removal of the shadow from copper.

‡ The second recension in the edition of Mangetus reads Sol throughout for Sal, but it is a printer's error.

excessively white. And know ye, that
the Flower of White Salt is Ethel
from Ethelia. The same must be
boiled for seven days, till it shall
become like gleaming marble, for when
it has reached this condition it is a
very great Arcanum, seeing that
Sulphur is mixed with Sulphur,
whence an excellent work is accomplished, by reason of the affinity
between them, because natures rejoice
in meeting their own natures. Take,
therefore, Mardek and whiten the same
with Gadenbe,* that is, wine and
vinegar, and Permanent Water. Roast
and coagulate until the whole does not
liquefy in a fire stronger than its own,
namely, the former fire. Cover the
mouth of the vessel securely, but let it
be associated with its neighbour, that it
may kindle the whiteness thereof, and
beware lest the fire blaze up, for in

---

* Though Martinus Rulandus endeavoured honestly
to explain all the barbarous terms of Alchemy in his
laborious lexicon, and though he was evidently well
acquainted with the *Turba*, he omits both Mardeck and
Gadenbe.

this case it becomes red prematurely, and this will profit you nothing, because in the beginning of the ruling you require the white. Afterwards coagulate the same until you attain the red. Let your fire be gentle in the whitening, until coagulation take place. Know that when it is coagulated we call it the Soul, and it is more quickly converted from nature into nature. This, therefore, is sufficient for those .who deal with the Art of Coins, because one thing makes it but many operate therein. For ye need not a number of things, but one thing only, which in each and every grade of your work is changed into another nature. *The* TURBA *saith*: Master, if you speak as the Wise have spoken, and that briefly, they will follow you who do not wish to be wholly shut in with darkness.

The Thirteenth Dictum.

PYTHAGORAS *saith*:—We posit another government which is not from another root, but it differs in name. And know, all ye seekers after this Science and Wisdom, that whatsoever the envious may have enjoined in their books concerning the composition of natures which agree together,* in savour there is only one, albeit to sight they are as diverse as possible. Know, also, that the thing which they have described in so many ways follows and attains its companion without fire, even as the magnet follows the iron, to which the said thing is not vainly compared, nor to a seed, nor to a matrix, for it is also like unto these. And this same thing, which follows† its companion without fire, causes many colours to appear when embracing it, for this reason, that the said one thing enters into every regimen, and is found everywhere, being a stone, and also not a stone; common and precious; hidden and concealed,

---

* The shorter recension reads: " concerning the harmony of the elements."

† According to the second recension, the subject in question causes many colours to appear in complexion, according as it is governed in every regimen.

yet known by everyone; of one name and of many names, which is the Spume of the Moon. This stone, therefore, is not a stone, because it is more precious; without it Nature never operates anything; its name is one, yet we have called it by many names on account of the excellence of its nature.*

The TURBA *answereth :*—O! Master! wilt thou not mention some of those

---

* Zosimus explains that the uncommunicated mystery which no one among the prophets has dared to divulge by word, but has revealed only to the initiates, is a process upon the stone Alabastron by means of vinegar. By the *Lexicon of Chrysopeia* in the Byzantine Collection—that earliest dictionary of alchemy, which has remained un-known to all later Hermetic lexicographers—Alabastron is defined to be the calx obtained from eggshells, saltpetre, a variety of natron, and common salt. The inquirer after the uncommunicated secret may take his choice among these substances, and it does not follow that the Lexicon is a correct exponent of Zosimus. However this may be, it appears that the stone Alabastron, either before or after the operation with vinegar, is the symbolical encephalous stone which is not a stone, the unknown thing which is known by all, the despised thing which is most precious, the thing given and not given by God. The preparation indicated is the Mythraic Mystery. The perplexities of the *Turba* at this point are, therefore, a device of the Greek alchemists, and they were fond of recurring to it.

names for the guidance of seekers?
And he :—It is called White Ethelia,
White Copper, and that which flies
from the fire and alone whitens copper.
Break up, therefore, the White Stone,
and afterwards coagulate it with milk.*
Then pound the calx in the mortar,
taking care that the humidity does
not escape from the vessel ; but coagulate it in the vessel until it shall become
a cinder. Cook also with Spume of
Luna and regulate. For ye shall find the
stone broken, and already imbued with
its own water.† This, therefore, is the
stone which we call by all names,
which assimilates the work and drinks
it, and is the stone out of which also
all colours appear. Take, therefore,
that same gum,‡ which is from the

---

* The second recension adds : "that is, after the manner
that milk is coagulated." The symbolical use of milk in
alchemy is, like so much of the terminology of the *Turba*,
of Greek origin. It will be found in the discourse of
Synesius.

† The second recension has a preferable reading : " Ye
shall find the stone formed, which imbue with its own
water."

‡ The second recension says : " Gum of Scotia," most

scoriæ, and mix with cinder of calx, which you have ruled, and with the fæces which you know, moistening with permanent water. Then look and see whether it has become a powder, but if not, roast in a fire stronger than the first fire, until it be pounded. Then imbue with permanent water, and the more the colours vary all the more suffer them to be heated. Know, moreover, that if you take white quicksilver, or the Spume of Luna, and do as ye are bidden, breaking up with a gentle fire, the same is coagulated, and becomes a stone. Out of this stone, therefore, when it is broken up, many colours will appear to you. But

---

probably a misprint for Scoria. Rulandus identifies philosophical gum with Ferment, Mercury, &c. The term is much used in alchemy, and is found in Zosimus, but without explanatory context. The *Turba Philosophorum* is not very clear on the subject of the philosophical gum, but it is as clear as the Greek Alchemists, for the *Lexicon of Chrysopeia* defines gum as the yolk of the egg, speaking philosophically and not literally; but the treatise on the *Nomenclature of the Egg* says that the white of egg is gum, among other things, speaking also philosophically, and without regard to the *Lexicon*.

herein, if any ambiguity occur to you
in our discourse, do as ye are bidden,
ruling the same until a white and
coruscating stone shall be produced,
and so ye find your purpose.

The Fourteenth Dictum.

ACSUBOFEN* *saith :* Master, thou hast
spoken without envy, even as became
thee, and for the same may God
reward thee! PYTHAGORAS *saith :* May
God also deliver thee, ACSUBOFEN,
from envy! *Then he :* Ye must know,
O Assembly of the Wise, that sulphurs
are contained in sulphurs, and humidity
in humidity.† *The* TURBA *answereth :*
The envious, O Acsubofen, have
uttered something like unto this! Tell
us, therefore, what is this humidity?
And he : Humidity is a venom, and
when venom‡ penetrates a body, it

---

* In the second recension the name is Assuberes.

† A Formula of the Greek Alchemists: Sulphurs are
mastered by Sulphurs, &c.

‡ The theriac and poison of the stone are favourite
subjects of discourse among early Latin Alchemists, like
Petrus Bonus and, indeed, the sovereign remedy
seems with all authors to have had a destructive as well as

tinges it with an invariable colour, and in no wise permits the soul to be separated from the body, because it is equal thereto. Concerning this, the envious have said: When one flies and the other pursues, then one seizes upon the other, and afterwards they no longer flee, because Nature has laid hold of its equal, after the manner of an enemy, and they destroy one another. For this reason, out of the sulphureous mixed sulphur is produced a most precious colour, which varies not, nor flees from the fire, when the soul enters into the interior of the body and holds the body together and tinges it. I will repeat my words in Tyrian dye.*   Take the Animal which is

---

a constructive aspect. A Syriac treatise, fixed by M. Berthelot as belonging to the tenth or eleventh century, says that "the elixir resembles a poison, because of its violence and subtlety," and Arabian alchemy contains many references to the *venenum ignis*. The Greek equivalent is *ios*, and this is recurring continually in the Byzantine Alchemical collection.

* This process, worded in the language of the Tyrian dye, may be compared with a similar recipe for the purple tincture, which occurs at the beginning of the *Natural and*

called Kenckel, since all its water is a Tyrian colour, and rule the same with a gentle fire, as is customary, until it shall become earth, in which there will be a little colour. But if you wish to obtain the Tyrian tincture, take the humidity which that thing has ejected, and place it therewith gradually in a vessel, adding that tincture whereof the colour was disagreeable to you. Then cook with that same marine water* until it shall become dry.† Afterwards moisten with that humour, dry gradually, and cease not to imbue it, to cook, and to dry, until it be imbued with all its humour. Then leave it for several days in its own vessel, until the most precious Tyrian colour shall come out from it to the surface. Observe how I describe the regimen to you! Prepare it with the urine of boys, with

---

Mystic Questions of Democritus. In this, also, urine plays an important part.

 * The use of sea water is specified in one of the Democritic treatises.

 † The second recension reads: " until it shall become moistened, after which evaporate the moisture."

water of the sea, and with permanent clean water, so that it may be tinged, and decoct with a gentle fire, until the blackness altogether shall depart from it, and it be easily pounded. Decoct, therefore, in its own humour until it clothe itself with a red colour. But if ye wish to bring it to the Tyrian colour, imbue the same with continual* water, and mix, as ye know to be sufficient, according to the rule of sight; mix the same with permanent water sufficiently, and decoct until rust absorb the water. Then wash with the water of the sea which thou hast prepared, which is water of desiccated calx;† cook until it imbibe its own moisture; and do this day by day. I tell you that a colour will thence appear to you the like of which the Tyrians have never made. And if ye wish that it should be a still more exalted colour, place the gum in the permanent water, with which ye shall dye it alternately, and

---

* The second recension reads: " with water of snow."
† The alternative reading is: water of talc.

afterwards desiccate in the sun. Then restore to the aforesaid water and the black Tyrian colour is intensified. But know that ye do not tinge the purple colour except by cold. Take, therefore, water which is of the nature of cold, and steep wool* therein until it extract the force of the tincture from the water. Know also that the Philosophers have called the force which proceeds from that water the Flower. Seek, therefore, your intent in the said water; therein place what is in the vessel for days and nights, until it be clothed with a most precious Tyrian colour.

The Fifteenth Dictum.

FRICTES *saith :*—O all ye seekers after Wisdom, know that the foundation of this Art, on account of which many have perished, is one only.† There is

---

* The second recension substitutes *Luna* for *Lana,* *i.e.,* Moon for wool.

† The one nature, the one matter, the one way, are all conceptions of Greek Alchemy. " The furnace is one, the way which must be followed is one, and one is also the

one thing which is stronger than all
natures, and more sublime in the
opinion of philosophers, whereas with
fools it is more common than anything.
But for us it is a thing which we
reverence. Woe unto all ye fools!
How ignorant are ye of this Art, for
which ye would die if ye knew it! I swear
to you that if kings were familiar with it,
none of us would ever attain this thing.
O how this nature changeth body into
spirit! O how admirable is Nature,
how she presides over all, and overcomes all! PYTHAGORAS *saith :*—Name
this Nature, O Frictes! *And he :*—It
is a very sharp vinegar,* which makes

work," says the *Assembly of the Philosophers*. " The ONE
furnishes blood to the OTHER, and the ONE engenders the
OTHER. Nature rejoices nature ; nature charms nature;
nature triumphs over nature ; nature masters nature ; and
this not for one such nature opposed to another such, but
for one only and same nature, proceeding by chemical
process from itself with pain and great labour."—*The
Serpent Ourobobos.*

    * The Greek *Assembly of the Philosophers* explains
that the philosophical vinegar is obtained by the coction of
the Stone. It appears to be an oil which rises to the
surface during the process, but the explanation is by no

gold into sheer spirit, without which vinegar, neither whiteness, nor blackness, nor redness, nor rust can be made. And know ye that when it is mixed with the body, it is contained therein, and becomes one therewith; it turns the same into a spirit, and tinges with a spiritual and invariable tincture, which is indelible. Know, also, that if ye place the body over the fire without vinegar, it will be burnt and corrupted. And know, further, that the first humour is cold. Be careful, therefore, of the fire, which is inimical to cold. Accordingly, the Wise have said: Rule gently until the sulphur becomes incombustible.* The Wise

---

means clear. M. Berthelot supposes a reference to the Mercurial Water.

* The Greek Alchemists give the following recipe for the production of incombustible sulphur: Take unburnt Sulphur, diluted in the urine of a person who has not reached puberty; then taking an equal quantity of brine, boil till the sulphur rises to the surface, and then it becomes incombustible. Prove it by reasoning and examining (? with fire) until it becomes incombustible, that is to say, until you see that it no longer burns. Take the same incombustible water (of sulphur), pour on flower of salt, dilute as

men have already shewn to those who possess reason the disposition of this Art, and the best point of their Art, which they mentioned, is, that a little of this sulphur burns a strong body. Accordingly they venerate it and name it in the beginning of their book, and the son of Adam thus described it. For this vinegar burns the body, converts it into a cinder, and also whitens the body, which, if ye cook well and deprive of blackness, is changed into a stone, so that it becomes a coin of most intense whiteness. Cook, therefore, the stone until it be disintegrated, and then dissolve and temper with water of the sea. Know also, that the beginning of the whole work is the whitening, to which succeeds the redness, finally the perfection of the work; but after this, by means of vinegar, and by the will of God, there follows a complete perfection. Now, I have shewn to you, O disciples of

---

in the case of the incombustible sulphur. This is the divine mystery.

this Turba, the disposition of the one thing, which is more perfect, more precious, and more honourable, than all natures, and I swear to you by God that I have searched for a long time in books so that I might arrive at the knowledge of this one thing, while I prayed also to God that he would teach me what it is. My prayer was heard, He shewed me clean water, whereby I knew pure vinegar, and the more I did read books, the more was I illuminated.

The Sixteenth Dictum.

SOCRATES *saith :*—Know, O crowd of those that still remain of the Sons of the Doctrine, that no tincture can be produced without Lead, which possesses the required virtue. Have ye not seen how thrice-great Hermes infused the red into the body, and it was changed into an invariable colour ?* Know, therefore, that the first virtue is vinegar,

---

* The second recension reads : " Have ye not seen, says thrice-great Hermes, that so often as it is infused into the body, the same body is changed into an invariable colour ? "

and the second is the Lead* of which the Wise have spoken, which if it be infused into all bodies, renders all unchangeable, and tinges them with an invariable colour. Take, therefore, Lead which is made out of the stone called Kuhul; † let it be of the best quality, and let it be cooked till it becomes black. Then pound the same with Water of Nitre until it is thick like grease, and cook again in a very bright fire until the spissitude of the body is destroyed,

---

* M. Berthelot tells us that lead was regarded by the Egyptian alchemists as the generator of the other metals and the first matter of transmutation, which he explains by the appearances it possesses in common with a number of other simple bodies and metallic alloys. Zosimus, the Panopolite, may be cited in confirmation of this point; he says : All substances were recognised by the Egyptians as produced by lead alone, for it is from lead that the three other bodies are derived, *i.e.,* copper, iron, and tin.—Zosimus *On the Substances and Non-substances of Art.*

† The significance of the term Kuhul, or more accurately Kohol, is to be found in Syriac alchemy; it is the equivalent of alcool and sulphurated antimony in the form of an impalpable powder. Kuhul, or Koheul, is explained by Rulandus to be the Lead of the Philosophers. The Alcohol mentioned by M. Berthelot seems to be different from Alcool of wine, and is, in fact, the pure part of any body separated from that which is impure.

the water being rejected. Kindle, therefore, above it until the stone becomes clean, abounding in precious metal, and exceedingly white. Pound it afterwards with dew and the sun, and with sea and rain water for 21 days, for 10 days with salt water, and 10 days with fresh water,* when ye shall find the same like to a metallic stone. Cook the same once more with water of nitre until it become tin by liquefaction. Again cook until it be deprived of moisture, and become dry. But know that when it becomes dry it drinks up what remains of its humour swiftly, because it is burnt lead. Take care, however, lest it be burnt. Thus we

---

* The second recension reads : " Afterwards pound it with dew, salt, and rain water for 29 days, again with salt water for 20 days, and yet again with fresh water for 10 days." The explanation of all Rosicrucian mysteries has been referred to the dew of the alchemists, and the *ros philosophorum* certainly plays an important part in the Great Mystery. In the *Natural and Mysterious Questions* of Democritus, dew is mentioned in connection with a process of whitening, and in the fragment on the *Philosophical Egg* it is tabulated as a name of the white or philosophical albumen, but here M. Berthelot suspects the additions of a later hand.

call it incombustible sulphur. Pound the same with the sharpest vinegar, and cook till it becomes thick, taking care lest the vinegar be changed into smoke and perish; continue this coction for 150 days. Now, therefore, I have demonstrated the disposition of the white lead, all which afterwards follows being no more than women's work and child's play. Know, also, that the arcanum of the work of gold proceeds out of the male and the female, but I have shewn you the male in the lead, while, in like manner, I have discovered for you the female in orpiment.* Mix, therefore, the orpiment with the lead, for the female rejoices in receiving the strength of the male, because she is assisted by the male. But the male receives a tingeing spirit from the female. Mix them, therefore,

---

* M. Berthelot indentifies orpiment with the arsenic of the ancients. The word itself does not occur in the Greek writers, but there is a fifteenth century translation from Latin to Greek of the *Semita Recta*, ascribed to Albertus Magnus, who reappears as Peter Theoctonicos, in which it is found.

together, place in a glass vessel, and
pound with Ethelia and very sharp
vinegar; cook for seven days, taking
care lest the arcanum smoke away, and
leave throughout the night. But if ye
wish it to put on mud (colour), seeing
that it is already dry, again imbue
with vinegar. Now, therefore, I have
notified to you the power of orpiment,
which is the woman by whom is accomplished the most great arcanum.
Do not shew these unto the evil, for
they will laugh. It is the Ethelia of
vinegar which is placed in the preparation, by which things God perfects the
work, whereby also spirits take
possession of bodies, and they become
spiritual.

The Seventeenth Dictum.

ZIMON* *saith :* O Turba of Philosophers and disciples, now hast thou
spoken about making into white, but it
yet remains to treat concerning the
reddening! Know, all ye seekers after

---

* Otherwise Zenon, according to the second recension.

this Art, that unless ye whiten, ye cannot make red, because the two natures are nothing other than red and white. Whiten, therefore, the red, and redden the white !* Know, also, that the year is divided into four seasons; the first season is of a frigid complexion, and this is Winter; the second is of the complexion of air, and this is Spring; then follows the third, which is summer, and is of the complexion of fire; lastly, there is the fourth, wherein fruits are matured, which is Autumn. In this manner, therefore, ye are to rule your natures, namely, to dissolve in winter, to cook in spring, to coagulate in summer, and to gather and tinge the fruit in autumn. Having, therefore, given this example, rule the tingeing natures, but if ye err, blame no one save yourselves. *The* TURBA *answereth:* Thou hast treated the matter extremely

---

* A commentary introduced into the text of Zosimus on Virtue and Interpretation, observes : If thou dost commence by making white, the yellowing will be perfect, perfect and solid.

well; add, therefore, another teaching
of this kind for the sake of posterity.
And he : I will speak of making lead
red.* Take the copper which
the Master ordered you to take
at the beginning of his book,
combine lead therewith, and cook it
until it becomes thick; congeal also
and desiccate until it becomes red.
Here certainly is the Red Lead of
which the wise spake ; copper and lead
become a precious stone ; mix them
equally, let gold be roasted with them,
for this, if ye rule well, becomes a
tingeing spirit in spirits.† So when
the male and the female are conjoined
there is not produced a volatile wife,
but a spiritual composite. From the
composite turned into a red spirit is
produced the beginning of the world.

---

* The various substances which alchemists confounded under the names of Minium, Rubric, etc., are
enumerated by M. Berthelot, including, in addition to the
sur-oxyde of lead, which is the modern name of minium,
not only vermillion, cinnabar, realgar, etc., but some
oxydes of iron.

† The second recension reads : "becomes a mighty
spirit among spirits."

Behold this is the lead which we have called Red Lead, which is of our work, and without which nothing is effected!

The Eighteenth Dictum.

MUNDUS *saith to the* TURBA: The seekers after this Art must know that the Philosophers in their books have described gum in many ways, but it is none other than permanent water, out of which our precious stone is generated.* O how many are the seekers after this gum, and how few there are who find it! Know that this gum is not ameliorated except by gold alone. For there be very many who investigate these applications, and they find certain things, yet they cannot sustain the labours because they are dimi-

---

* It appears from Zosimus on *The Detailed Exposition of the Work*, that with the addition of a little [philosophical] gum any species of body may be tinged. And when Mundus identifies Gum with Permanent Water he is in agreement with the same authority, for in the context of the passage just cited we find the following words: That which tinges tinctures and things tinged is Divine water, the great mystery. The gum of gold is mentioned in a fragment attributed to Agathodemon.

nished. But the applications which are made out of the gum and out of the honourable stone, which has already held the tincture, they sustain the labours, and are never diminished. Understand, therefore, my words, for I will explain unto you the applications of this gum, and the arcanum existing therein. Know ye that our gum is stronger than gold, and all those who know it do hold it more honourable than gold, yet gold we also honour, for without it the gum cannot be improved. Our gum, therefore, is for Philosophers more precious and more sublime than pearls, because out of gum with a little gold we buy much. Consequently, the Philosophers, when committing these things to writing that the same might not perish, have not set forth in their books the manifest disposition, lest every one should become acquainted therewith, and having become familiar to fools, the same would not sell it at a small price. Take, therefore, one part of the most intense white gum ;

one part of the urine of a white calf; one part of the gall of a fish; and one part of the body of gum, without which it cannot be improved; mix these portions and cook for forty days. When these things have been done, congeal by the heat of the sun till they are dried. Then cook the same, mixed with milk of ferment, until the milk fail; afterwards extract it, and until it become dry evaporate the moisture by heat. Then mix it with milk of the fig, and cook it till that moisture be dried up in the composite, which afterwards mix with milk of the root of grass, and again cook until it be dry. Then moisten it with rainwater, then sprinkle with water of dew, and cook until it be dried. Also imbue with permanent water, and desiccate until it become of the most intense dryness. Having done these things, mix the same with the gum which is equipped with all manner of colours, and cook strongly until the whole force of the water perish; and the entire body be deprived of its humidity, while ye imbue the same by cooking, until the dryness thereof be kindled. Then dismiss for forty days. Let it remain in that trituration or decocting until the spirit penetrate the body. For by this regimen the spirit is made corporeal, and the body is changed into a spirit. Observe the vessel, therefore, lest the composition fly and pass off in fumes. These things being accomplished, open the vessel, and ye will find that which ye purposed. This, therefore, is the arcanum of gum, which the Philosophers have concealed in their books.

The Nineteenth Dictum.

DARDARIS *saith :* It is common knowledge that the Masters* before us have described Permanent Water. Now, it behoves one who is introduced to this Art to attempt nothing till he is familiar with the power of this Per-

---

* The reference to the Masters, which occurs twice in this dictum, is to be understood not of previous speakers in the Assembly, but of the older philosophers, namely, the Greek Alchemists.

manent Water, and in commixture, contrition, and the whole regimen, it behoves us to use invariably this famous Permanent Water. He, therefore, who does not understand Permanent Water, and its indispensable regimen, may not enter into this Art, because nothing is effected without the Permanent Water. The force thereof is a spiritual blood, whence the Philosophers have called it Permanent Water, for, having pounded it with the body, as the Masters before me have explained to you, by the will of God it turns that body into spirit.* For these, being mixed together and reduced to one, transform each other; the body incorporates the spirit, and the spirit incorporates the body into tinged spirit, like blood. And know ye, that whatsoever hath spirit the same hath blood also as well. Remember, therefore, this arcanum !

---

* The second recension adds: "and the spirit into body."

The Twentieth Dictum.

BELUS *saith :*—O disciples, ye have discoursed excellently !* PYTHAGORAS *answers :*—Seeing that they are philosophers, O Belus, why hast thou called them disciples ? *He answereth :*—It is in honour of their Master, lest I should make them equal with him. *Then* PYTHAGORAS *saith :*—Those who, in conjunction with us, have composed this book which is called the *Turba*, ought not to be termed disciples. *Then he :*— Master, they have frequently described Permanent Water, and the making of

---

* The whole of this Dictum recalls a passage in Zosimus, *On Virtue and Interpretation.*—It is for these reasons that my excellent master, Democritus, makes himself the following distinction ; "Take that stone which is not a stone, that precious thing which has no value, that polymorphous object which is without form, that unknown thing which is known to everyone, which has many names and has no name, I refer to aphroselinon." For this stone is not a stone, and while it is exceedingly precious, at the same time it has no money value; its nature is one, its name one. Nevertheless, many denominations have been given it, I do not say absolutely speaking, but according to its nature, so that whether it is called the being which flees the fire, or white smoke, or white copper, no falsehood is uttered.

the White and the Red in many ways,
albeit under many names; but in the
modes after which they have conjoined
weights, compositions, and regimens,
they agree with the hidden truth.
Behold, what is said concerning this
despised thing! A report has gone
abroad that the Hidden Glory of the
Philosophers is a stone and not a stone,
and that it is called by many names,
lest the foolish should recognise it.
Certain wise men have designated it
after one fashion, namely, according
to the place where it is generated;
others have adopted another, founded
upon its colour, some of whom have
termed it the Green Stone;* by other
some it is called the Stone of the most
intense Spirit of Brass, not to be mixed
with bodies; by yet others its description has been further varied, because
it is sold for coins by lapidaries who
are called *saven;* some have named it
Spume of Luna;† some have distin-

---

* The second recension reads: " Green Lion."

† Sputum Lunæ does not seem to be a term which
found favour with Latin alchemy, and accordingly it is

guished it astronomically or arithmetically; it has already received a thousand titles, of which the best is :—
" That which is produced out of metals." So also others have called it the Heart of the Sun, and yet others have declared it to be that which is brought forth out of quicksilver with the milk of volatile things.

The Twenty-first Dictum.

PANDOLFUS *saith :*—O Belus, thou hast said so much concerning the despised

---

wanting in the Lexicons. It is very curious to note that Rulandus, who quite frequently quotes the *Turba,* seems seldom to have troubled himself about the significance of its bizarre terms. In Zosimus, *On Virtue and Interpretation,* there is a prescription from Hermes concerning " that which falls from the moon when it is waning," and he is referred to as describing where it is to be found, and how it has the quality of resisting the fire. In fact, says Hermes, " you will find it with me and with Agathodaimon." M. Berthelot supposes this passage to allegorise upon the volatilisation of mercury. But the expression in the *Turba* recalls the passage of Synesius. Note also the mythology of Selenite, Lapis Arabicus, Aphroselinum, &c., supposed not only to reflect the likeness of the Moon, but to be " made from dew by the foam of the Moon."— *Rulandus.*

stone* that thou hast left nothing to be
added by thy brethren! Howsoever,
I teach posterity that this despised
stone is a permanent water, and know,
all ye seekers after Wisdom, that permanent water is water of mundane
life,† because, verily, Philosophers have
stated that Nature rejoices in Nature,
Nature contains Nature, and Nature
overcomes Nature. The Philosophers
have constituted this short dictum the
principle of the work for reasonable
persons. And know ye that no body
is more precious or purer than the Sun,
and that no tingeing venom‡ is gene-

---

* The Turba Philosophorum does not betray any-
where the hand of a Christian compiler, and although the
reference to the despised stone suggests the stone which
the builders have rejected, the idea is derived from
Zosimus, and not from the New Testament, except in so far
as Zosimus himself may have drawn it from that source.
Treating, in his dictum on the subject of calx, concerning
the uncommunicated mystery of the encephalous stone,
the Greek adept calls it the despised thing which is most
precious, and so on through a number of contradicting
denominations.

† The second recension reads: "clean water."

‡ The symbolism of the venom of the philosophers is
also found in Zosimus, commenting upon Democritus.

rated without the Sun and its shadow.
He, therefore, who attempts to make
the venom of the Philosophers without
these, already errs, and has fallen into
that pit wherein his sadness remains.
But he who has tinged the venom of
the wise out of the Sun and its shadow*
has arrived at the highest Arcanum.
Know also that our coin when it
becomes red, is called gold; he, therefore, who knows the hidden Cambar†
of the Philosophers, to him is the
Arcanum already revealed. *The* TURBA
answereth :—Thou hast even now intel-

The Greek word signifies, says an annotation of
M. Berthelot, the *rouille* of metals, the specific virtue
of bodies, and the venom of serpents. According to
Zosimus, it is the spirit separated from the substance of a
body.—*On Virtue and Interpretation.*

* A quotation from Mary (the first) in Zosimus *On the
Measure of Yellowing* runs thus:—Copper when burned
with sulphur, treated with oil ot natron, and recovered
after having undergone the same process several times,
becomes an excellent gold without shadow.

† This oriental term is referred to by M. Berthelot in
his *Essay on the Transmission of Ancient Science* without
explanation of its significance, and it is not found in any
of the Lexicons of Alchemy. In an ancient alchemical
treatise, entitled *The Code of Truth*, it figures as the name
of an adept.

ligibly described this stone, yet thou
hast not narrated its regimen nor its
composition. Return, therefore, to the
description. *He saith :*—I direct you
to take an occult and honourable arcanum, which is White Magnesia,* and
the same is mixed and pounded with
wine, but take care not to make use
of this except it be pure and clean;
finally place it in its vessel, and pray God
that He may grant you the sight of this
very great stone.† Then cook gradually,
and, extracting, see if it has become a
black stone, in which case ye have
ruled excellently well. But rule it thus
for the white, which is a great arcanum,
until it becomes Kuhul, closed up with

---

* The *Chemistry of Moses* gives the following process
for the whitening of Magnesia:—" Taking Magnesia and
an equal quantity of Cappadocian salt, place in a vessel of
burnt clay. Let it stay there from evening till morning.
Then, if it be black, let it be cooked till it whitens, but it
is far better to cook it in a glass-maker's furnace. Hide
this mystery, for it comprises everything which concerns
whitening by decoction."

† It does not appear that the conception of the
Philosopher's Stone as a medicine of metals and of men
was familiar to Greek alchemy.

blackness, which blackness see that it does not remain longer than forty days. Pound the same, therefore, with its confections, which are the said flower of copper, gold of the Indies whose root is one, and a certain extract of an unguent, that is, of a crocus, that is, fixed exalted alum, or ♄ ;* cook the four, therefore, permanently for 40 or 42 days. After these days God will show you the principle (or beginning) of this stone, which is the stone Atitos, of which favoured sight of God there are many accounts. Cook strongly, and imbue with the gum that remains. And know ye that so often as ye imbue the cinder, so often must it be desiccated and again humectated, until its colour turns into that which ye desire. Now, therefore, will I complete that which I have

---

* The authenticity of this sign is extremely doubtful, and the marginal note which is appended to most printed editions does not help it out. It is no doubt really a misreading of the word *Hoc*, which is required to make sense of the sentence immediately following. The second recension confirms this view.

begun, if God will look kindly on us.* Know also that the perfection of the work of this precious stone is to rule it with the residue of the third part of the medicine, and to preserve the two other parts for imbuing and cooking alternately till the required colour appears.† Let the fire be more intense than the former; let the matter be cerated, and when it is desiccated it coheres. Cook, therefore, the wax until it imbibes the gluten of gold, which being desiccated, imbue the rest of the work seven times until the other two-thirds be finished, and true earth imbibe them all. Finally, place the same on a hot fire until the earth extract its flower and be satisfactory. Blessed are ye if ye understand! But, if not, I will repeat to you the perfection of

---

* The original is untranslatable; the conjectural emendation given in the text has no authority, and is only introduced to provide a meaning.

† The reading of the second recension has been substituted, owing to the corrupt state of the longer text.

the work. Take the clean white, which is a most great arcanum, wherein is the true tincture; imbue sand therewith, which sand is made out of the stone seven times imbued, until it drink up the whole, and close the mouth of the vessel effectually, as you have often been told. For that which ye seek of it by the favour of God, will appear to you, which is the stone of Tyrian colour. Now, therefore, I have fulfilled the truth, so do I conjure you by God and your sure Master, that you show not this great arcanum, and beware of the wicked!

The Twenty-Second Dictum.

THEOPHILUS *saith:* Thou hast spoken intelligently and elegantly, and art held free from envy. *Saith the* TURBA: Let your discretion, therefore, explain to us what the instructing Pandolfus has stated, and be not envious. *Then he :* O all ye seekers after this science, the arcanum of gold and the art of the coin is a dark vestment, and no one knows what the Philosophers have narrated in their books without frequent reading, experiments, and questionings of the Wise. For that which they have concealed is more sublime and obscure than it is possible to make known in words, and albeit some have dealt with it intelligibly and well, certain others have treated it obscurely; thus some are more lucid than others. *The* TURBA *answereth:* Thou hast truly spoken. *And he:* I announce to posterity that between boritis and copper there is an affinity, because the boritis of the Wise liquefies the copper, and it changes as a fluxible water. Divide, therefore, the venom into two equal parts, with one of which liquefy the copper, but preserve the other to pound and imbue the same, until it is drawn out into plates; cook again with the former part of the venom, cook two to seven in two; cook to seven in its own water for 42 days;*

---

* This unintelligible passage is better rendered in the first recension :—" Cook with the former part of the venom

finally, open the vessel, and ye shall find copper turned into quicksilver; wash the same by cooking until it be deprived of its blackness, and become as copper without a shadow. Lastly, cook it continuously until it be congealed. For when it is congealed it becomes a very great arcanum. Accordingly, the Philosophers have called this stone Boritis;* cook, therefore, that coagulated stone until it becomes a matter like mucra. Then imbue it with the Permanent water which I directed you to reserve, that is to say, with the other portion, and cook it many times until its colours manifest. This, therefore, is the very great putrefaction which extracts (or contains in itself) the very great arcanum. *Saith the* TURBA:

---

until it shall have absorbed both, and do this seven times." But *donec duas ebibat* does not agree with the subsequent directions found in each version.

* Boritis, according to Rulandus, is the White Stone after the black state, and it reduces earth to water. A late French Lexicon observes that the name was applied by Philosophers to their Mercury when it had reached the extreme black stage. It is the Laton which must be whitened. The word is of Oriental origin.

Return to thine exposition, O Theophilus! *And he:* It is to be known that the same affinity which exists between the magnet and iron, also exists assuredly between copper and permanent water. If, therefore, ye rule copper and permanent water as I have directed, there will thence result the very great arcanum in the following fashion. Take white Magnesia and quicksilver,* mix with the male, and pound strongly by cooking, not with the hands, until the water become thin. But dividing this water into two parts, in the one part of the water cook it for eleven, otherwise, forty days, until there be a white flower, as the flower of salt in its splendour and coruscation: but strongly close the mouth of the vessel, and cook for forty days, when ye will find it water whiter than milk; deprive it of all blackness by cooking; continue the cooking until its whole nature be disintegrated, until the de-

---

* The second recension reads:—" Take quicksilver mixed with the male."

filement perish, until it be found clean, and is wholly broken up (or becomes wholly clean). But if ye wish that the whole arcanum, which I have given you, be accomplished, wash the same with water, that is to say, the other part which I counselled you to preserve, until there appear a crocus, and leave in its own vessel. For the Iksir pounds (or contains) itself; imbue also with the residue of the water, until by decoction and by water it be pounded and become like a syrup of pomegranates; imbue it, therefore, and cook, until the weight of the humidity shall fail, and the colour which the Philosophers have magnified shall truly appear.

The Twenty-third Dictum.

CERUS* *saith :* Understand, all ye Sons of the Doctrine, that which Theophilus hath told you, namely, that there exists an affinity between the magnet and the

---

* The name substituted by the second recension is Bellus.

iron, by the alliance of composites existing between the magnet and the iron, while the copper is fitly ruled for one hundred days :* what statement can be more useful to you than that there is no affinity between tin† and quicksilver ?‡ *The* TURBA *answereth :* Thou hast ill spoken, having disparaged the true disposition. *And he :* I testify that I say nothing but what is true ; why are you incensed against me ? Fear the Lord, all ye Turba, that your Master may believe you ! *The* TURBA *answereth :* Say what you will. *And he :* I direct you to take quicksilver, in which is the male potency§ or strength ;

---

* The second recension adds :—" Between the copper and water of the Philosophers. This affinity and combination is given to them in the space of one hundred days."

† The definition may not be important, but it is, perhaps, as well to state that the Greek *Lexicon of Chrysopœia* explains that tin alchemically is cinnabar, and that cinnabar is sublimed vapour obtained by coction in cauldrons. Here M. Berthelot observes that the reference is to sublimed mercury or the sulphur thereof.

‡ According to the alternative version :—" The nature of the one does not agree with the nature of the other."

§ " The proper end of the whole art," says Horus, " is to obtain the semen of the male secretly, seeing that all

cook the same with its body until it becomes a fluxible water; cook the masculine together with the vapour, until each shall be coagulated and become a stone. Then take the water which you had divided into two parts, of which one is for liquefying and cooking the body, but the second is for cleansing that which is already burnt, and its companion, which [two] are made one. Imbue the stone seven times, and cleanse, until it be disintegrated, and its body be purged from all defilement, and become earth. Know also that in the time of forty-two days the whole is changed into earth; by cooking, therefore, liquefy the same until it become as true water, which is quicksilver. Then wash with water of nitre until it become as a liquefied coin. Then cook until it be congealed and become like to tin, when it is a most

---

things are male and female. Hence Horus says in a certain place: Join the male and the female, and you will find that which is sought; as a fact, without this process of reunion, nothing can succeed, for Nature charms Nature," &c.—Olympiodorus *On the Sacred Art.*

great arcanum; that is to say, the stone which is out of two things. Rule the same by cooking and pounding, until it becomes a most excellent crocus. Know also that unto water desiccated with its companion we have given the name of crocus. Cook it, therefore, and imbue with the residual water reserved by you until you attain your purpose.

The Twenty-fourth Dictum.

BOCASCUS* *saith*: Thou hast spoken well, O Belus, and therefore I follow thy steps! *He answereth :* As it may please you, but do not become envious, for that is not the part of the Wise. *And* BOCASCUS: Thou speakest the truth, and thus, therefore, I direct the Sons of the Doctrine. Take lead, and, as the Philosophers have ordained, imbue, liquefy, and afterwards congeal, until a stone is produced; then rule the stone with gluten of gold and syrup of pome-granates until it be broken up. But you

* The name in the second recension is Boratis.

G

have already divided the water into two parts, with one of which you have liquefied the lead, and it has become as water; cook, therefore, the same until it be dried and have become earth; then pound with the water reserved until it acquire a red colour, as you have been frequently ordered.* *The* TURBA *answereth :* Thou hast done nothing but pile up ambiguous words. Return, therefore, to the subject. *And he :* Ye who wish to coagulate quick-silver,† must mix it with its equal.‡

---

* Otherwise: " Rule frequently, as I have said."

† The Greek alchemists claim to have accomplished the fixation of Mercury by means of the Body of Magnesia, by which Zosimus understands molybdochalchos. An unassigned fragment of the Byzantine collection has the following poetical reference to the fixation of Mercury :—
" Mercury is obtained in like manner with artificial cinnabar, a rare substance, that is, one met with rarely. I refer to cinnabar obtained by the dry way and a suitable roasting. It is that above all which is termed dried and easily volatilised, employed in the testing of souls. Having become an etherised spirit, it darts towards the upper hemisphere ; it descends and ascends, avoiding the action of the fire, until, quitting its *rôle* of fugitive, it reaches a state of wisdom. Until it has attained this condition, it is difficult to retain, and is mortal."—*Fabrication of the All.*

‡ " With its body," says the second recension ; it is a printer's choice between *compari* and *corpori.*

Afterwards cook it diligently until both
become permanent water, and, again,
cook this water until it be coagulated.
But let this be desiccated with its own
equal vapour, because ye have found
the whole quicksilver to be coagulated
by itself.* If ye understand, and place
in your vessel what is necessary, cook
it until it be coagulated, and then
pound† until it becomes a crocus like to
the colour of gold.

The Twenty-fifth Dictum.

MENABDUS *saith:* May God reward thee
for the regimen, since thou speakest
the truth! For thou hast illuminated
thy words. *And they :* It is said because
thou praisest him for his sayings, do
not be inferior to him. *And he :* I know
that I can utter nothing but that which
he hath uttered ; however, I counsel
posterity to make bodies not bodies,

---

* The second recension reads:—" Let the whole be
coagulated into quicksilver."

† The second recension merely says :—" Place it once
more in its vessel, and pound."

but these incorporeal things bodies.* For by this regimen the composite is prepared, and the hidden part of its nature is extracted. With these bodies accordingly join quicksilver and the body of Magnesia,† the woman also with the man, and by means of this there is extracted our secret Ethelia, through which bodies are coloured; assuredly, if I understand this regimen, bodies become not bodies, and incorporeal things become bodies. If ye diligently pound the things in the fire and digest

---

* The Byzantine fragment upon *The Philosophical Egg* contains this statement: "Unless bodies lose their corporeal state, and unless bodies again assume their corporeal state, that which is desired will not be attained." But Mary is quoted by Olympiodorus in terms which correspond literally with the text of the *Turba*: "Except you convert corporeal substances into incorporeal, and incorporeal substances into corporeal, and unless you make two bodies into one body, no desired result will be achieved." The "divine" Zozimus also quotes Hermes in precisely the same fashion, and he observes elsewhere that to convert and transmute is to impart body to the incorporeal.—*The Body of Magnesia.*

† Zosimus, commenting upon Mary, concludes that the Body of Magnesia is molybdochalchos, or black lead. [See note on p. 82.] The confusion of old chemistry on the subject of the last substance is well known.

(or join to) the Ethelias, they become clean and fixed things. And know ye that quicksilver is a fire burning the bodies, mortifying and breaking up, with one regimen, and the more it is mixed and pounded with the body, the more the body is disintegrated, while the quicksilver is attenuated and becomes living. For when ye shall diligently pound fiery quicksilver and cook it as required, ye will possess Ethel, a fixed nature* and colour, subject to every tincture, which also overcomes, breaks, and constrains the fire.† For this reason it does not colour things unless it be coloured, and being coloured it colours.‡ And know that no body can tinge itself unless its spirit be extracted from the secret belly thereof, when it becomes a body and soul with-

---

* That is, according to the second recension, "one which does not flee from the fire."

† Alternatively, "all bodies," which seems a preferable reading.

‡ The second recension says that "it holds and colours all spirits, because Ethelia tinges all things when once it has been itself tinged."

out the spirit,* which is a spiritual tincture, out of which colours have manifested, seeing that a dense thing does not tinge a tenuous, but a tenuous nature colours that which enters into a body. When, however, ye have ruled the body of copper, and have extracted from it a most tenuous (subject), then the latter is changed into a tincture by which it is coloured.† Hence has the wise man said, that copper does not tinge unless first it be tinged. And know that those four bodies which you

---

* This distinction between the soul and the spirit is recognised by Zosimus, who follows Democritus. The soul is the primitively sulphureous and caustic nature. The purifying influence of fire preserves the spirit when the operation has been conducted according to the rules of Art. The spirit is the useful part, the tingeing element.— *The Four Metallic Bodies, &c.*

† In his treatise *On Virtue and Interpretation*, Zosimus cites Democritus to the effect that copper does not tinge, but that copper burnt by means of oil of natron, and having undergone this treatment repeatedly, becomes more beautiful than gold. "Copper does not tinge so long as it preserves an unique essence, but it tinges by its combination with other bodies. How then, if this combination be wanting, and before the copper has been tinged, can one succeed in tingeing objects made subject to the action of fire?"

are directed to rule are this copper, and that the tinctures which I have signified unto you are the condensed and the humid,* but the condensed is a conjoined vapour, and the humid is the water of sulphur, for sulphurs are contained by sulphurs, and rightly by these things Nature rejoices in Nature, and overcomes, and constrains.

The Twenty-Sixth Dictum.

ZENON *saith:* I perceive that you, O crowd of the Wise, have conjoined two bodies, which your Master by no means ordered you to do! *The* TURBA *answereth:* Inform us according to your own opinion, O Zenon, in this matter, and beware of envy! *Then he:* Know that the colours which shall appear to you out of it are these. Know, O Sons of the Doctrine, that it behoves you to allow the composition to putrefy for forty days, and then to

---

* The second recension reads: "The condensed and the humid are these two tinctures, the condensed being joined with the humid."

sublimate five times in a vessel. Next
join to a fire of dung, and cook, when
these colours shall appear to you : On
the first day black citrine, on the
second black red, on the third like
unto a dry crocus,* finally, the purple
colour will appear to you ; the ferment
and the coin of the vulgar shall be
imposed ; then is the Ixir composed
out of the humid and the dry, and
then it tinges with an invariable tincture. Know also that it is called a body
wherein there is gold.   But when ye
are composing the Ixir, beware lest
you extract the same hastily, for it
lingers.†   Extract, therefore, the same
as an Ixir.   For this venom is, as it
were, birth and life, because it is a
soul extracted out of many things, and
imposed upon coins :‡ its tincture,

---

* The preferable reading is: "Crocus like unto
sericus."

† The second recension substitutes : " Beware lest
you extract the spirit in haste, for perchance it will
perish."

‡ The second recension reads :—" And the soul shall
remain, a tincture extracted out of many things, and
imposed upon coins."

therefore, is life to those things with which it is joined, from which it removes evil, but it is death to the bodies from which it is extracted. Accordingly, the Masters have said that between them there exists the same desire as between male and female, and if any one, being introduced to this Art, should know these natures, he would sustain the tediousness of cooking until he gained his purpose according to the will of God.

The Twenty-Seventh Dictum.

GREGORIUS* *saith :* O all ye Turba, it is to be observed that the envious have called the venerable stone Efflucidinus,† and they have ordered it to be ruled until it coruscates like marble in its splendour.‡ *And*

---

* The name in the second recension is Chambar.

† Antimony, in the second recension. The most bizarre terms of the *Turba* did not find favour with Western Alchemists ; Efflucidinus is a special instance in point. It is difficult to speak with complete authority, but it may be said almost certainly that no later author made use of it. Moreover, no vocabulary mentions it.

‡ The comparison of the Stone in its splendour to gleaming marble is found, among other of the Greek

they: Show, therefore, what it is to posterity. *Then he*: Willingly; you must know that the copper is commingled with vinegar, and ruled until it becomes water. Finally, let it be congealed, and it remains a coruscating stone with a brilliancy like marble, which, when ye see thus, I direct you to rule until it becomes red, because when it is cooked till it is disintegrated and becomes earth, it is turned into a red colour. When ye see it thus, repeatedly cook and imbue it until it assume the aforesaid colour, and it shall become hidden gold. Then repeat the process, when it will become gold of a Tyrian colour. It behoves you, therefore, O all ye investigators of

---

alchemists, in Zosimus, and especially in his *Detailed Exposition of the Work*, where, however, he is quoting Democritus. "Mark the Philosopher, seized with a divine transport, on the subject of this white sulphur: If the preparation become like unto marble, then is there a great mystery." And again, having cited Stephanus, he proceeds: "Now, that which tinges tinctures and tinged substances, the same is divine water, the great mystery, which is like unto marble."

this Art, when ye have observed that this Stone is coruscating, to pound and turn it into earth, until it acquires some degree of redness ; then take the remainder* of the water which the envious† ordered you to divide into two parts, and ye shall imbibe them‡ several times until the colours which are hidden by no body appear unto you.§ Know also that if ye rule it ignorantly, ye shall see nothing of those colours. I knew a certain person who commenced this work, and operated the natures of truth, who, when the redness was somewhat slow in appearing, imagined that he had made a mistake, and so relinquished the work.‖ Observe, therefore, how ye make the conjunc-

---

* Otherwise: "a small quantity."

† The opprobrious term is omitted by the second recension, and the reference seems to be to the division of the water indicated in an earlier part of the colloquy.

‡ The second recension substitutes "sand."

§ Otherwise: "until the hidden colours shall appear."

‖ A common anecdote of the alchemists, reproduced with many variations, and even in Hermetic poems, such as Norton's *Ordinal of Alchemy*.

tion, for the punic dye,* having embraced his spouse, passes swiftly into
her body, liquefies, congeals, breaks
up, and disintegrates the same. Finally,
the redness does not delay in coming,
and if ye effect it without the weight,
death will take place, whereupon it
will be thought to be bad.   Hence, I
order that the fire should be gentle in
liquefaction, but when it is turned to
earth make the same intense,† and
imbue it until God shall extract the
colours for us and they appear.

The Twenty-eighth Dictum.

CUSTOS *saith :* I am surprised, O all ye
Turba ! at the very great force and
nature of this water, for when it has
entered into the said body, it turns it
first into earth, and next into powder,
to test the perfection of which take in
the hand, and if ye find it impalpable
as water, it is then most excellent ;

---

* The second recension reads : " the male."

† That is, "intenser in congelation," according to
the second recension.

otherwise, repeat the cooking until it is brought to the required condition. And know that if ye use any substance other than our copper, and rule with our water, it will profit you nothing. If, on the other hand, ye rule our copper with our water, ye shall find all that has been promised by us. *But the* Turba *answereth:* Father, the envious* created no little obscurity when they commanded us to take lead and white quicksilver, and to rule the same with dew and the sun till it becomes a coin-like stone. *Then he:* They meant our copper and our permanent water, when they thus directed you to cook in a gentle fire, and affirmed that there should be produced the said coin-like stone, concerning which the Wise have also observed, that Nature rejoices in Nature, by reason of the affinity which they know to exist between the

---

* The distinction between the Wise and the Envious is a little difficult to follow, nor is it at all certain that the envious had less wisdom than the wise, or the wise less envy than the envious. In either case, they were all Greeks indifferently.

two bodies, that is to say, copper and permanent water. Therefore, the nature of these two is one, for between them there is a mixed affinity, without which they would not so swiftly unite, and be held together so that they may become one. *Saith the* TURBA: Why do the envious direct us to take the copper which we have now made, and roasted until it has become gold?

The Twenty-Ninth Dictum.

DIAMEDES *saith :* Thou hast spoken already, O Moses*, in an ungrudging manner, as became thee; I will also confirm thy words, passing over the hardness of the elements which the wise desire to remove, this disposition being most precious in their eyes. Know, O ye seekers after this doctrine, that man does not proceed except from a man ; that only which is like unto themselves is begotten from brute animals ; and so also with flying creatures.

---

* This reference is omitted from the second recension. Moses may be a misprint for Custos, or *vice versa.*

I have treated these matters in compendious fashion, exalting you towards the truth, who yourselves omit prolixity, for Nature is truly not improved by Nature, save with her own nature, seeing that thou thyself art not improved except in thy son, that is to say, man in man.* See, therefore, that ye do not neglect the precepts concerning her, but make use of venerable Nature, for out of her Art cometh, and

---

* " When thou hast attained, my child, to the understanding of these things by way of a preliminary, consider creation and generation as a whole, and know that man is able to bring forth man, the lion begets the lion, and the dog procreates the dog. Should it happen that a creature is produced contrary to nature, it is a monster which is engendered, and the same hath no consistence. Nature charms nature, and nature triumphs through nature. The adepts having participated in the divine power, and having succeeded by the divine assistance, illuminated by the fruit of the prayers of Isis, made preparations with certain metallic minera, without having recourse to other (unsuitable) substances. Thus they succeeded by means of the substantial nature in triumphing over the matter employed in the preparations. In fact, even as I have previously said that wheat begets wheat, and man sows man, so also gold serves for the increase of gold, and like things generally for the reproduction of their like. Now hath the mystery been revealed."— *Isis to Horus.*

out of no other. Know also that unless you seize hold of this Nature and
rule it, ye will obtain nothing. Join,
therefore, that male, who is son to
the red slave,* in marriage with his
fragrant wife, which having been done,
Art is produced between them; add no
foreign matter unto these things,
neither powder nor anything else; that
conception is sufficient for us, for it is
near, yet the son is nearer still.† How
exceeding precious is the nature of

---

* The allegory of the *Servus Fugitivus* abounds in
later alchemy, and is found also in old Arabian treatises,
such as the *Twelve Chapters of Ostanes*: "They have
defined this Stone by saying that it is running water and
permanent water; burning fire and frozen fire; dead
earth; hard stone and soft stone. It is the flying slave,
the swift and the stable; the thing which makes and is
made," &c. In the *Speculum Majus* of Vincent de
Beauvais it appears as a synonym of Mercury, which of
course is an obvious symbolism. Rulandus attributes it to
some treatise ascribed to Hermes. According to other
lexicons, the Red Servant is the matter from which the
Philosophers extract their Mercury, which must therefore
be the marriageable son mentioned in the text above. The
fugitive *rôle* of Mercury is referred to in the Greek fragment on *The Fabrication of the All,* as already cited.

† The second recension reads: "A true son is
begotten."

that red slave, without which the
regimen cannot endure ! BACSEN *saith* :
O Diomedes, thou hast publicly revealed this disposition ! *He answereth* :
I will even shed more light upon it.
Woe unto you who fear not God, for
He may deprive you of this art !
Why, therefore, are you envious
towards your brethren ? *They answer* :
We do not flee except from fools ; tell
us, therefore, what is thy will ? *And he* :
Place Citrine with his wife after the
conjunction into the bath ; do not
kindle the bath excessively, lest they
be deprived of sense and motion ;
cause them to remain in the bath until
their body, and the colour thereof,
shall become a certain unity, whereupon restore unto it the sweat thereof ;
again suffer it to die ; then give it rest,
and beware lest ye evaporate them by
burning them in too strong a fire.
Venerate the king and his wife,* and

---

* According to Rulandus, the King is the spiritual
water which gives moisture to the female, but there are
many meanings. This passage is the fountain-head of the
whole symbolism of the alchemical marriage, which is

H

do not burn them, since you know not when you may have need of these things, which improve the king and his wife. Cook them, therefore, until they become black, then white, afterwards red, and finally until a tingeing venom is produced. O seekers after this Science, happy are ye, if ye understand, but if not, I have still performed my duty, and that briefly, so that if ye remain ignorant, it is God who hath concealed the truth from you! Blame not, therefore, the Wise, but yourselves, for if God knew that ye possessed a faithful mind, most certainly he would reveal unto you the truth. Behold, I have established you therein, and have extricated you from error!

The Thirtieth Dictum.

BACSEN *saith:* Thou hast spoken well, O Diomedes, but I do not see that

---

concerned; always with royal personages. Compare the *Sponsus* and *Sponsa* of the *Chemical Nuptials of Christian Rosy Cross*, and the innumerable pictorial emblems which illustrate Latin Alchemy. It does not appear to be traceable to a Greek source.

thou hast demonstrated the disposition
of Corsufle* to posterity! Of this same
Corsufle the envious have spoken
in many ways, and have confused it
with all manner of names. *Then he:*
Tell me, therefore, O Bacsen, according to thy opinion in these
matters, and I swear by thy father
that this is the head of the work,† for
the true beginning hereof cometh after
the completion. BACSEN *saith:* I give
notice, therefore, to future seekers
after this Art, that Corsufle is a composite, and that it must be roasted

---

* The lexicographers of alchemy who followed
Rulandus after a long interval, explain that Corsufle, or as
they sometimes wrote it, Carsufle, is the Sulphur of the
Philosophers fixed at the Red Stage. Under neither form
is the term to be found in Rulandus himself, though he
was well acquainted with the *Turba.* His dictionary,
however, includes Cor Fuffla, which might be a mutilated
version produced in a German printing office. It signifies
the impurity of bodies, a definition which does not
correspond either with the text of the *Turba,* or with the
subsequent vocabularies. The origin of the word is
obscure, and it is not found in the collections of Arabian
or Syrian alchemy published by M. Berthelot.

† According to the second recension, Corsufle is the
head, *i.e.,* the crown, and not the beginning of the work.
The speaker also is different, namely, Nephitus.

seven times, because when it arrives at perfection it tinges the whole body. *The* TURBA *answereth :*—Thou hast spoken the truth, O Bacsen!

The Thirty-First Dictum.

PYTHAGORAS *saith :*—How does the discourse of Bacsen appear to you, since he has omitted to name the substance by its artificial names? *And they*: Name it, therefore, oh Pythagoras! *And he :* Corsufle being its composition, they have applied to it all the names of bodies in the world, as, for example, those of coin, copper, tin, gold, iron, and also the name of lead, until it be deprived of that colour and become Ixir. *The* TURBA *answereth :* Thou hast spoken well, O Pythagoras! *And he :* Ye have also spoken well, and some among the others may discourse concerning the residual matters.

The Thirty-Second Dictum.

BONELLUS *saith :* According to thee, O Pythagoras, all things die and live

by the will of God, because that nature
from which the humidity is removed,
that nature which is left by nights,
does indeed seem like unto something
that is dead; it is then turned and
(again) left for certain nights, as a man
is left in his tomb, when it becomes a
powder.*   These things being done,
God will restore unto it both the soul
and the spirit thereof, and the weak-
ness being taken away, that matter will
be made strong, and after corruption
will be improved, even as a man
becomes stronger after resurrection and
younger than he was in this world.
Therefore it behoves you, O ye Sons
of the Doctrine, to consume that
matter with fire boldly until it shall
become a cinder, when know that ye
have mixed it excellently well, for that
cinder receives the spirit, and is imbued

---

* The text is corrupt and unintelligible. The second
recension reads: "Therefore that nature from which the
humidity has been removed, when it has been left for
nights, is like to one dead; and then that nature is wanting
in fire until the spirit of that body returns; and then it
becomes dust like unto one dead in his tomb."

with the humour until it assumes a
fairer colour than it previously possessed. Consider, therefore, O ye Sons
of the Doctrine, that artists are unable
to paint with their own tinctures until
they convert them into a powder;
similarly, the philosophers cannot combine medicines for the sick slaves until
they also turn them into powder, cooking some of them to a cinder, while
others they grind with their hands.
The case is the same with those who
compose the images of the ancients.
But if ye understand what has already
been said, ye will know that I speak
the truth, and hence I have ordered
you to burn up the body and turn it
into a cinder, for if ye rule it subtly
many things will proceed from it, even
as much proceeds from the smallest
things in the world. It is thus because
copper like man, has a body and a
soul, for the inspiration of men cometh
from the air, which after God is their
life, and similarly the copper is inspired
by the humour from which that same

copper receiving strength is multiplied and augmented like other things. Hence, the philosophers add, that when copper is consumed with fire and iterated several times, it becomes better than it was. *The Turba answereth* : Show, therefore, O Bonellus, to future generations after what manner it becometh better than it was! *And he :* I will do so willingly ; it is because it is augmented and multiplied, and because God extracts many things out of one thing, since He hath created nothing which wants its own regimen, and those qualities by which its healing must be effected. Similarly, our copper, when it is first cooked, becomes water ; then the more it is cooked, the more is it thickened until it becomes a stone, as the envious have termed it, but it is really an egg tending to become a metal. It is afterwards broken and imbued, when ye must roast it in a fire more intense than the former, until it shall be coloured and shall become like blood in combustion, when it is placed on coins and changes them into gold, according to the Divine pleasure. Do you not see that sperm is not produced from the blood unless it be diligently cooked in the liver till it has acquired an intense red colour, after which no change takes place in that sperm ?* It is the same with our work, for unless it be cooked diligently until it shall become a powder, and afterwards be putrefied until it shall become a spiritual sperm, there will in no wise proceed from it that colour which ye desire. But if ye arrive at the conclusion of this regimen, and so obtain your purpose, ye shall be princes among the people of your time.

The Thirty-Third Dictum.

NICARUS *saith :*—Now ye have made this arcanum public. *The* TURBA

---

* The comparison of the progress of the work to the development of the embryo, which is suggested by the above reference, and is, in fact, common to all Latin adepts, is found also in the Greek writers, and among

answereth : Thus did the Master order. *And he :* Not the whole, nevertheless. *But they :* He ordered us to clear away the darkness therefrom ; do thou, therefore, tell us. *And he :* I counsel posterity to take the gold which they wish to multiply and renovate, then to divide the water into two parts. *And they :* Distinguish, therefore, when they divide the water. *But he :* It behoves them to burn up our copper with one part. For the said copper, dissolved in that water, is called the ferment of Gold,* if

---

these, in Comarius, who says that the test of fire nourishes the material as the embryo is nourished in the mother's womb.

* M. Berthelot traces the original notion of the fermentation of metals to the sophistication called *diplosis*. "Recipes designed for the accomplishment of a more profound imitation are also met with, for example, the alliance of gold or silver with a more or less considerable quantity ot some less precious metal; this was the operation of *diplosis*." It is found in the Leyden papyrus, but there are traces that the Egyptian goldsmith believed, or at any rate sought to make others believe, "that the true metal was really multiplied by an operation comparable to fermentation." The fermentation of metals is mentioned in many places by the Greek writers: "It is necessary that this water, after the manner of leaven, should determine the fermentations destined to produce the like, by

ye rule well. For the same in like manner are cooked and liquefy as water; finally, by cooking they are congealed, crumble, and the red appears. But then it behoves you to imbue seven times with the residual water, until they absorb all the water, and, all the moisture being dried up, they are turned into dry earth; then kindle a fire and place therein for forty days until the whole shall putrefy, and its colours appear.

The Thirty-Fourth Dictum.

BACSEN *saith*: On account of thy dicta the Philosophers said beware.* Take the regal Corsufle, which is like to the redness of copper, and pound in the urine of a calf until the nature

---

means of the like, in the metallic body to be tinged. As a fact, after the same manner that the leaven of dough, used in a small quantity, ferments a great mass of paste, so also will this little morsel of gold ferment all the dry matter." This notion is repeated in terms essential and literal by innumerable Latin alchemists.

* For this somewhat bizarre reading the second recension substitutes : " It seems needful to lay stress upon some matters which have been already mentioned."

of the Corsufle is converted, for the true nature has been hidden in the belly of the Corsufle. *The* TURBA *saith*: Explain to posterity what the nature is. *And he*: A tingeing spirit which it hath from permanent water, which is coinlike, and coruscates. *And they*: Shew, therefore, how it is extracted. *And he*: It is pounded, and water is poured upon it seven times until it absorbs the whole humour, and receives a force which is equal to the hostility of the fire; then it is called rust. Putrefy the same diligently until it becomes a spiritual powder, of a colour like burnt blood, which the fire overcoming hath introduced into the receptive belly of Nature, and hath coloured with an indelible colour. This, therefore, have kings sought, but not found, save only to whom God has granted it.* *But*

---

* It was different in the days of Zosimus, who tells us that in Egypt the divine art of operating on minera belonged to the Kings, and the alchemists of the Nile no more worked in their own interest than the minters of coin. The increase of the King's riches was the only end in view,

the TURBA *saith*: Finish your speech,
O Bacsen. *And he*: I direct them to
whiten copper with white water, by
which also they make red. Be careful
not to introduce any foreign matter.
And the TURBA: Well hast thou
spoken, O Bacsen, and Nictimerus
also has spoken well! *Then he*: If I
have spoken well, do one of you
continue.

The Thirty-Fifth Dictum.

But ZIMON * *saith*: Hast thou left anything to be said by another? *And the*
TURBA: Since the words of Nicarus and
Bacsen are of little good to those who
seek after this Art, tell us, therefore,
what thou knowest, according as we
have said. *And he:* Ye speak the
truth, O all ye seekers after this Art!
Nothing else has led you into error but
the sayings of the envious,† because what

and for this reason the priests who were acquainted with
the mineral secrets did not dare to disclose them publicly.

* In the second recension the name is rendered
Zeunon.

† The second recension has an important variation:
" The words of the Egyptians have led us into error."

ye seek is sold at the smallest possible price.* If men knew this, and how great was the thing they held in their hands, they would in no wise sell it. Therefore, the Philosophers have glorified that venom,† have treated of it variously, and in many ways, have taken and applied to it all manner of names, wherefore, certain envious persons have said: It is a stone and not a stone, but a gum of Ascotia, consequently, the Philosophers have concealed the power thereof. For this spirit which ye seek, that ye may tinge therewith, is concealed in the body, and hidden away from sight, even as the soul in the human body.‡ But ye

---

* This passage recalls many statements to the same effect in the Greek alchemists, as, for example, that the end is not to be obtained by money, "for the Lord God has delivered the same gratuitously, by reason of the beggars and the despairing." But this passage from the Byzantine *Assembly of the Philosophers* is in part at least an interpolation.

† The second recension reads: "that useful and abject thing."

‡ Otherwise: "Therein is the spirit which you seek, which tinges, vivifies, gives health and life to bodies."

seekers after the Art, unless ye disintegrate this body, imbue and pound
both cautiously and diligently, until
ye extract it from its grossness (or
grease), and turn it into a tenuous and
impalpable spirit, have your labour in
vain. Wherefore the Philosophers have
said : Except ye turn bodies into not-
bodies, and incorporeal things into
bodies, ye have not yet discovered the
rule of operation. *But the* TURBA
saith : Tell, therefore, posterity how
bodies are turned into not-bodies.
And he : They are pounded with fire
and Ethelia till they become a
powder.* And know that this does
not take place except by an exceedingly strong decoction, and continuous contrition, performed with
a moderate fire,† not with hands,‡

---

* The second recension reads : " When Ethelia is
pounded until it becomes dust," but it is evidently corrupt.

† The counsel of Olympiodorus is similar : " The fire
must burn with moderation and gentleness, lest the vapour
should escape in smoke and be lost," And, again : " Know
that this Art is not practised by means of a fierce fire."

‡ Some Latin alchemists say that the *Magnum Opus*
is a work of the hands, which others deny, and a very pretty

with imbibition and putrefaction, with exposure to the sun and to Ethelia. The envious caused the vulgar to err in this Art when they stated that the thing is common in its nature and is sold at a small price. They further said that the nature was more precious than all natures, wherefore they deceived those who had recourse to their books. At the same time they spoke the truth, and therefore doubt not these things. *But the* TURBA *answereth :* Seeing that thou believest the sayings of the envious, explain, therefore, to posterity the disposition of the two natures. *And he :* I testify to you that Art requires two natures, for the precious is not produced without the common,

---

diversity of opinion has risen up among interpreters in consequence. The partisans of the first view, denying the metallic object of the Art, affirm that the mystery of the manual operation was the mystery of animal magnetism. The *Turba* in the passage above, and in other places, is against the use of the hands, whatever that may have signified, here following Olympiodorus: "Think not thou, as do some, that manual action is of itself and alone sufficient ; there is also required that of Nature, an action superior to man's."—*On the Sacred Art.*

nor the common without the precious.
It behoves you, therefore, O all ye
investigators of this Art, to follow the
sayings of Victimerus,* when he said
to his disciples: Nothing else helps
you save to sublimate water and
vapour. *And the* Turba : The whole
work is in the vapour and the sublimation of water. Demonstrate, therefore, to them the disposition of the
vapour. *And he :* When ye shall perceive that the natures have become
water by reason of the heat of the
fire, and that they have been purified,
and that the whole body of Magnesia
is liquefied as water; then all things
have been made vapour, and rightly,
for then the vapour contains its own
equal, wherefore the envious† call either
vapour, because both are joined
in decoctions, and one contains the
other. Thus our stag finds no path to
escape, although flight be essential to

---

* " Of the elders," says the second recension.

† The second recension substitutes " The Philosophers," a variation which, in its way, is significant.

it. The one keeps back the other, so that it has no opportunity to fly, and it finds no place to escape ; hence all are made permanent, for when the one falls, being hidden in the body, it is congealed with it, and its colour varies, and it extracts its nature from the properties which God has infused into His elect, and it alienates it, lest it flee. But the blackness and redness appear, and it falls into sickness, and dies by rust and putrefaction ; properly speaking, then, it has not a flight, although it is desirous to escape servitude ; then when it is free it follows its spouse, that a favourable colour may befall itself and its spouse ; its beauty is not as it was, but when it is placed with coins, it makes them gold. For this reason, therefore, the Philosophers have called the spirit and the soul vapour. They have also called it the black humid wanting perlution ; and forasmuch as in man there are both humidity and dryness, thus our work, which the envious have concealed, is nothing else

I

but vapour and water. *The* TURBA *answereth* : Demonstrate vapour and water! *And he* : I say that the work is out of two ; the envious have called it composed out of two, because these two become four, wherein are dryness and humidity, spirit and vapour. *The* TURBA *answereth* : Thou hast spoken excellently, and without envy. Let Zimon next follow.

The Thirty-Sixth Dictum.

AFFLONTUS,* the Philosopher, *saith:* I notify to you all, O ye investigators of this Art, that unless ye sublime the substances at the commencement by cooking, without contrition of hands, until the whole become water, ye have not yet found the work. And know ye, that the copper was formerly called sand, but by others stone, and, indeed, the names vary in every regimen. Know further, that the nature and humidity become water, then a stone, if ye cause them to be

---

* The name in the second recension is Assotes.

well complexionated, and if ye are acquainted with the natures, because the part which is light and spiritual rises to the top, but that which is thick and heavy remains below in the vessel. Now this is the contrition of the Philosophers, namely, that which is not sublimated sinks down, but that which becomes a spiritual powder rises to the top of the vessel, and this is the contrition of decoction, not of hands. Know also, that unless ye have turned all into powder, ye have not yet pounded them completely. Cook them, therefore, successively until they become converted, and a powder. Wherefore Agadaimon*

---

* Agathodaimon is included among the makers of gold in one of the earlier sections of the Byzantine collection. He is quoted by Olympiodorus (*On the Sacred Art*), and a short account of him is given by the same writer. "It is stated by some that he was a man ancient among the most ancient who philosophised in Egypt, by others that he is a mysterious angel, or that he is the good genius of Egypt," &c. M. Berthelot points out that there was an Egyptian divinity who bore a name equivalent to this. Zosimus beheld Agathodaimon in a vision when his soul ascended to the third degree. An *Explanation and Com-*

saith : Cook the copper until it become a gentle and impalpable body, and impose in its own vessel; then sublimate the same six or seven times until the water shall descend. And know that when the water has become powder then has it been ground diligently. But if ye ask, how is the water made a powder ? note that the intention of the Philosophers is that the body before which before it falls into the water is not water may become water ; the said water is mixed with the other water, and they become one water. It is to be stated, therefore, that unless ye turn the thing mentioned into water,* ye shall not attain to the work. It is, therefore, necessary for the body to be so possessed by the flame of the fire that it is disintegrated and becomes weak with the water, when the water has been

mentary of Agathodaimon upon the Oracle of Orpheus is extant in the Greek collection.

* The second recension reads: " unless ye turn both into water."

added to the water, until the whole becomes water. But fools, hearing of water, think that this is water of the clouds. Had they read our books they would know that it is permanent water, which cannot become permanent without its companion, wherewith it is made one. But this is the water which the Philosophers have called Water of Gold, the Igneous, Good Venom, and that Sand of Many Names which Hermes ordered to be washed frequently, so that the blackness of the Sun might be removed, which he introduced in the solution of the body. And know, all ye seekers after this Art, that unless ye take this pure body, that is, our copper without the spirit, ye will by no means see what ye desire, because no foreign thing enters therein, nor does anything enter unless it be pure. Therefore, all ye seekers after this Art, dismiss the multitude of obscure names, for the nature is one water; if anyone err, he draws nigh to destruction, and loses his life. Therefore, keep this one nature, but dismiss what is foreign.

The Thirty-Seventh Dictum.

BONELLUS *saith*: I will speak a little concerning Magnesia. *The* TURBA *answereth*: Speak. *And he*: O all ye Sons of the Doctrine, when mixing Magnesia, place it in its vessel, the mouth of which close carefully, and cook with a gentle fire until it liquefy, and all become water therein! For the heat of the water acting thereupon, it becomes water by the will of God. When ye see that the said water is about to become black, ye know that the body is already liquefied. Place again in its vessel, and cook for forty days, until it drink up the moisture of the vinegar and honey.*   But certain

---

* There is an exceedingly curious reference to honey in the Discourse of Synesius. The question being what is the difference between the mercury which is obtained from cinnabar, and that which is obtained from arsenic, the Philosopher explains that while all mercury is one, there are still a variety of sorts, and he quotes Hermes:—
" The ray of honey is white," and " the ray of honey is

persons uncover it, say, once in each week, or once in every ten nights; in either case, the ultimate perfection of pure water appears at the end of forty days, for then it completely absorbs the humour of the decoction. Therefore, wash the same, and deprive of its blackness, until, the blackness being removed, the stone becomes dry to the touch. Hence the envious have said: Wash the Magnesia with soft water, and cook diligently, until it become earth, and the humour perish. Then it is called copper. Subsequently, pour very sharp vinegar upon it, and leave it to be soaked therein. But this is our copper, which the Philosophers have ordained should be washed with permanent water, wherefore they have said: Let the venom *

---

yellow." M. Berthelot explains that honey signifies mercury, which in the special connection is of course obvious, but it does not follow that this is the significance which was invariably attached to it by the philosophers. As a fact, in later days the term was used to signify the philosophical dissolvent.

* The following explanation is given by M. Berthelot. The Greek Ios, and Virus, the Latin equivalent, are words

be divided into two parts, with one of which burn up the body, and with the other putrefy. And know, all ye seekers after this Science, that the whole work and regimen does not take place except by water, wherefore, they say that the thing which ye seek is one, and, unless that which improves it be present in the said thing, what ye look for shall in no wise take place. Therefore, it behoves you to add those things which are needful, that ye may thereby obtain that which you purpose. *The* TURBA *answereth:* Thou has spoken excellently, O Bonellus! If it please thee, therefore, finish that which thou art saying; otherwise repeat it a second time. *But he:* Shall I indeed repeat these and like things? O all ye in-

---

which had exceedingly diverse meaning among the ancients. The Virus, according to Pliny, meant certain properties or specific virtues of bodies, such as the odour of copper, ivory, and sandarac; the medical action of calx of gold; the magnetic virtue communicated to iron by the magnet." Hence the term signified the power and not the operation, or if the operation, then this in all its phases, whether of healing or hurting. Ios also signified in a special way the oxyde of metals.

vestigators of this Art, take our copper; place with the first part of the water in the vessel; cook for forty days; purify from all uncleanliness; cook further until its days be accomplished, and it become a stone having no moisture. Then cook until nothing remains except fæces.* This done, cleanse seven times, wash with water, and when the water is used up leave it to putrefy in its vessel, so long as may seem desirable to your purpose. But the envious called this composition when it is turned into blackness *that which is sufficiently black*, and have said: Rule the same with vinegar and nitre. But that which remained when it had been whitened they called *sufficiently white*, and ordained that it should be ruled with permanent water. Again, when

---

* The whole mystery is in the scoriæ," says Zosimus, in *The Diversity of Burnt Copper*, and though the remark has a particular application, it was also with alchemists of the nature of a general axiom. So Olympiodorus: "In fact, the negative body *par excellence*, that which is called black lead, that which the Egyptian prophets desired to know, that which the oracles of the demons have revealed, all these are the scoriæ and cinders of Mary."

they called the same *sufficiently red*, they ordained that it should be ruled with water and fire until it became red.   *The* TURBA *answereth* : Show forth unto posterity what they intended by these things.   *And he* : They called it *Ixir satis*, by reason of the variation of its colours.   In the work, however, there is neither variety, multiplicity, nor opposition of substances ; it is necessary only to make the black copper white and then red.   However, the truth-speaking Philosophers had no other intention than that of liquefying, pounding, and cooking Ixir until the stone should become like unto marble in its splendour.   Accordingly, the envious again said : Cook the same with vapour until the stone becomes coruscating by reason of its brilliancy. But when ye see it thus, it is, indeed, the most great Arcanum.   Notwithstanding, ye must then pound and wash it seven times with permanent water ; finally, again pound and congeal in its own water, until ye extract its own concealed nature. Wherefore, saith Maria, sulphurs are contained in sulphurs, but humour in like humour, and out of sulphur mixed with sulphur, there comes forth a great work. But I ordain that you rule the same with dew * and the sun, until your purpose appear to you. For I signify unto you that there are two kinds of whitening and of making red, of which one consists in rust† and the other in contrition and decoction. But ye do

---

*The Greek alchemists assumed a special virtue in dew, but it was not apparently so much inherent in the moisture itself, as in the rays of the morning sun with which it is chiefly connected. Neither alchemically or otherwise was the night dew ever considered beneficial. Democritus, in the *Rational and Mystical Questions*, says : " Whiten this earth with sea water or sweetened saumur, or with the water of heaven : I mean by exposing it to dew and the sun," &c. There seems no special reason why this should not be understood literally. In the *Turba Philosophorum*, dew appears under another aspect, as possessing an inherent virtue apart from the vital presence and activity of the solar rays. In Latin alchemy, however, the references to dew are not very frequent, and it does not seem to have played so important a part in the symbolism of the adepts as Mosheim and others have supposed.

† Or, according to the second recension, " in making red."

not need any contrition of hands. Beware, however, of making a separation from the waters lest the poisons get at you, and the body perish with the other things which are in the vessel.†

The Thirty-Eighth Dictum.

EFFISTUS *saith:* Thou hast spoken most excellently, O Bonellus, and I bear witness to all thy words! *The* TURBA *saith:* Tell us if there be any service in the speech of Bonellus, so that those initiated in this disposition may be more bold and certain. EFFISTUS *saith:* Consider, all ye investigators of this Art, how Hermes, chief of the Philosophers, spoke and demonstrated when he wished to mix the natures. Take, he tells us, the stone of gold, combine with humour which is permanent water, set in its vessel, over a gentle fire until liquefaction

---

† Otherwise, "the body and soul which are in the vessel shall quickly perish."

takes place. Then leave it until the water dries, and the sand and water are combined, one with another; then let the fire be more intense than before, until it again becomes dry, and is made earth. When this is done, understand that here is the beginning of the arcanum; but do this many times, until two-thirds of the water perish, and colours manifest unto you. *The* TURBA *answereth:* Thou hast spoken excellently, O Effistus! Yet, briefly inform us further. *And he:* I testify to posterity that the dealbation doth not take place save by decoction.* Consequently, Agadaimon has very properly treated of cooking, of pounding, and of imbuing,†

---

* The Greek equivalent of Decoction identifies the process with that cooking which is so often ordained in all alchemical experiments. In the *New Light* of Arnoldus de Villa Nova three grades of the operation are described, together with the special furnaces and appliances required. In the first grade, the matter becomes black; in the second, white; and in the third, red. The description is accompanied in each case by a citation from the *Turba*.

† The second recension substitutes: "for which cause there must be frequent pounding and imbuing."

ethelia. Yet I direct you not to pour on the whole of the water at one time, lest the Ixir be submerged, but pour it in gradually, pound and dessicate, and do this several times until the water be exhausted. Now concerning this the envious have said: Leave the water when it has all been poured in, and it will sink to the bottom. But their intention is this, that while the humour is drying, and when it has been turned into powder, leave it in its glass vessel for forty days, until it passes through various colours, which the Philosophers have described. By this method of cooking the bodies put on their spirits and spiritual tinctures, and become warm.* *The* TURBA *answereth:* Thou hast given light to us, O Effistus, and hast done excellently! Truly art thou cleared from envy; wherefore, let one of you others speak as he pleases.

---

* The second recension reads: "bodies become spirits, and the spirits are made hot, and they tinge."

The Thirty-Ninth Dictum.

BACSEN *saith :** O all ye seekers after this Art, ye can reach no useful result without a patient, laborious,† and solicitous soul, persevering courage, and continuous regimen. He, therefore, who is willing to persevere in this disposition, and would enjoy the result, may enter upon it, but he who desires to learn over speedily, must not have recourse to our books, for they impose great labour before they are read in their higher sense, once, twice, or thrice. Therefore, the Master *saith*: Whosoever bends his back over the study of our books, devoting his leisure thereto,

---

* The speaker in the second recension is called Admion.

† The like exhortation is met with everywhere in the literature of the adepts. "Patience and delay are indispensable in our magistery. Haste, indeed, is of the devil's part in this magistery."—*Rosary of the Philosophers.* And again, "It is impossible for this to be known by the seeker unless he learns it from God, or from the instruction of a master. Know also that the way is very long; therefore are patience and delay needful in this our magistery."—*Ibid.*

is not occupied with vain thoughts, but fears God, and shall reign in the Kingdom without fail until he die.* For what ye seek is not of small price. Woe unto you who seek the very great and compensating treasure of God! Know ye not that for the smallest purpose in the world, earthly men will give themselves to death, and what, therefore, ought they to do for this most excellent and almost impossible offering? Now, the regimen is greater than is perceived by reason, except through divine inspiration. I once met with a person who was as well

---

* The fear of God has always been regarded as essential to the success of the true alchemist. The explanation is to be sought in the fact that the operations of nature were a region of awe and wonder to early experiment. The Greek alchemists regarded no operation as possible without the divine concurrence, and Zosimus says : " Abide at thine own fireside acknowledging but one God and one Art; do not deviate in search of another God; for God will come to thee, He who is present everywhere. . . . . Rest thy body, and hush thy passions; so, governing thyself, thou shalt call unto thee the Divine Being, and the Divine Being will come to thee. . . . When thou shalt know thyself, then shalt thou know also the only God existing in thee ; and acting thus thou shalt attain truth and nature, rejecting matter with contempt."

acquainted with the elements as I myself, but when he proceeded to rule this disposition, he attained not to the joy thereof by reason of his sadness and ignorance in ruling, and excessive eagerness, desire, and haste concerning the purpose. Woe unto you, sons of the Doctrine! For one who plants trees does not look for fruit, save in due season; he also who sows seeds does not expect to reap, except at harvest time. How, then, should ye desire to attain this offering when ye have read but a single book, or have adventured only the first regimen? But the Philosophers have plainly stated that the truth is not to be discerned except after error, and nothing creates greater pain at heart than error in this Art, while each imagines that he has almost the whole world, and yet finds nothing in his hands. Woe unto you! Understand the dictum of the Philosopher, and how he divided the work when he said—pound, cook, reiterate, and be

K

thou not weary. But when thus he divided the work, he signified commingling, cooking, assimilating, roasting, heating, whitening, pounding, cooking Ethelia, making rust or redness, and tingeing. Here, therefore, are there many names, and yet there is one regimen. And if men knew that one decoction and one contrition would suffice them, they would not so often repeat their words, as they have done, and in order that the mixed body may be pounded and cooked diligently, have admonished you not to be weary thereof. Having darkened the matter to you with their words, it suffices me to speak in this manner. It is needful to complexionate the venom rightly, then cook many times, and do not grow tired of the decoction. Imbue and cook it until it shall become as I have ordained that it should be ruled by you—namely, impalpable spirits, and until ye perceive that the Ixir is clad in the garment of the Kingdom. For when ye behold the Ixir turned into

Tyrian colour,* then have ye found that which the Philosophers discovered before you.† If ye understand my words (and although my words be dead, yet is there life therein for those who understand themselves), they will forthwith explain any ambiguity occurring herein. Read, therefore, repeatedly, for reading is a dead speech, but that which is uttered with the lips the same is living speech. Hence we have ordered you to read frequently, and, moreover, ponder diligently over the things which we have narrated.

The Fortieth Dictum.

JARGUS *saith :* Thou hast left obscure a part of thy discourse, O Bacsen ! *And he :* Do thou, therefore, Jargus, in thy clemency shew forth the same !

---

* Latin alchemists made use of the symbolism of Tyrian dye when describing the Red state of the Magistery. The Kenckel, previously referred to, is apparently an Eastern term designating the crustacea from the shells of which the dye was anciently obtained.

† The second recension reads : "then shall ye comprehend the sayings of the Philosophers."

And he answereth : The copper of which thou hast before spoken is not copper, nor is it the tin of the vulgar ; it is our true work (or body) which must be combined with the body of Magnesia, that it may be cooked and pounded without wearying until the stone is made. Afterwards, that stone must be pounded in its vessel with the water of nitre, and, subsequently, placed in liquefaction until it is destroyed. But, all ye investigators of this art, it is necessary to have a water by which the more you cook, so much the more you sprinkle,* until the said copper shall put on rust, which is the foundation of our work. Cook, therefore, and pound with Egyptian vinegar.

The Forty-First Dictum.

Zimon† *saith :* Whatsoever thou hast uttered, O Jargos, is true, yet I do

---

* The second recension reads : " It is necessary to use a water which becomes inspissated in proportion as it is cooked."

† In the second recension the name is Cadmon.

not see that the whole Turba hath spoken concerning the rotundum.* *Then he:* Speak, therefore, thine opinion concerning it, O Zimon! ZIMON *saith:* I notify to posterity that the rotundum turns into four elements, and is derived out of one thing.†

The TURBA *answereth:* Inasmuch as thou art speaking, explain for future generations the method of ruling. *And he:* Willingly: it is necessary to take one part of our copper, but of Permanent Water three parts; then let them be mixed and cooked until they be thickened and become one stone, concerning which the envious have said: Take one part of the pure body, but three parts of copper of Magnesia; then commingle with

---

* The term rotundum used in this curious manner is to be understood of the Stone. The *Scala Philosophorum* speaks of "our perfect tyriac and rotund stone," the four elements being concordantly exalted in the quality of the temperate stone.

† There is a variation in the second recension: "I signify to future generations that the rotundum which converts copper into four is from one thing."

rectified vinegar, mixed with male of earth; close the vessel, observe what is in it, and cook continuously until it becomes earth.

The Forty-Second Dictum.

ASCANIUS *saith:* Too much talking, O all ye Sons of the Doctrine, leads this subject further into error! But when ye read in the books of the Philosophers that Nature is one only, and that she overcomes all things: Know that they are one thing and one composite. Do ye not see that the complexion of a man is formed out of a soul and body; thus, also, must ye conjoin these, because the Philosophers, when they prepared the matters and conjoined spouses mutually in love with each other, behold there ascended from them a golden water! *The* TURBA *answereth:* When thou wast treating of the first work, lo! thou didst turn unto the second! How ambiguous hast thou made thy book, and how obscure are thy words!

Then he : I will perform the disposition of the first work. *The* TURBA *answereth :* Do this. *And he* : Stir up war between copper and quicksilver, until they go to destruction and are corrupted, because when the copper conceives the quicksilver it coagulates it, but when the quicksilver conceives the copper, the copper is congealed into earth; stir up, therefore, a fight between them; destroy the body of the copper until it becomes a powder. But conjoin the male to the female, which are vapour* and quicksilver, until the male and the female become Ethel, for he who changes them into spirit by means

---

* The Latin alchemists regarded vapour as the first matter of all things, and in a special way it was the First Matter of the Philosophers. The *Rosary of the Philosophers* observes : "The first matter of bodies is not the mercury of the vulgar, but is an unctuous and humid vapour. The mineral stone is made from the humid, and the metallic body from the unctuous. It is needful that bodies should be converted into such an unctuous vapour, and they are destroyed, brought to nothing, and mortified in the conversion, and this is accomplished by means of our white and red water." But this unctuous vapour was the mercury of the philosophers and wise men.

of Ethel, and next makes them red, tinges every body, because, when by diligent cooking ye pound the body, ye extract a pure, spiritual, and sublime soul therefrom, which tinges every body. *The* TURBA *answereth:* Inform, therefore, posterity what is that body. *And he:* It is a natural sulphureous thing* which is called by the names of all bodies.

The Forty-Third Dictum.

DARDARIS *saith:* Ye have frequently treated of the regimen, and have introduced the conjunction,† yet I proclaim to posterity that they cannot extract the now hidden soul except by Ethelia, by which bodies become not bodies through continual cooking, and by sublimation of Ethelia. Know also that quicksilver is fiery, burning every body more than does fire, also mortifying

---

* The second recension reads: "sulphur of nature," concerning which much is found in later alchemical writers.

† According to the second recension: "much has been said of the regimen but of the conjunction little."

bodies, and that every body which is mingled with it is ground and delivered over to be destroyed. When, therefore, ye have diligently pounded the bodies, and have exalted them as required, therefrom is produced that Ethel nature, and a colour which is tingeing* and not volatile, and it tinges the copper which the Turba said did not tinge until it is tinged, because that which is tinged tinges. Know also that the body of the copper is ruled by Magnesia, and that quicksilver is four bodies, also that the matter has no being except by humidity, because it is the water of sulphur, for sulphurs are contained in sulphurs. *The* TURBA *saith:* O Dardaris, inform posterity what sulphurs are ! *And he* : Sulphurs are souls which are hidden in four bodies, and, extracted by themselves, do contain one another, and are naturally conjoined. For if ye rule that which is hidden in the belly of sulphur with water, and cleanse well that which

---

*Otherwise : " not fleeing from the fire."

is hidden, then nature rejoices, meeting with nature, and water similarly with its equal. Know ye also that the four bodies are not tinged but tinge.* *And the* TURBA: Why dost thou not say like the ancients that when they are tinged, they tinge? *And he*: I state that the four coins of the vulgar populace are not tinged, but they tinge copper, and when that copper is tinged, it tinges the coins of the populace.†

The Forty-Fourth Dictum.

MOYSES *saith*: This one thing of which thou hast told us, O Dardaris, the Philosophers have called by many names, sometimes by two and sometimes by three names! DARDARIS *answereth*: Name it, therefore, for posterity, setting aside envy. *And he*: The one is that which is fiery, the two is the

---

* According to the second recension, "they tinge a fifth."

† According to the second recension, they are not tinged, "except copper, which then tinges the coins of the vulgar."

body composed in it, the three is the water of sulphur, with which also it is washed and ruled until it be perfected. Do ye not see what the Philosopher affirms, that the quicksilver which tinges gold is quicksilver out of Cambar? DARDARIS *answereth :* What dost thou mean by this? For the Philosopher says : sometimes from Cambar and sometimes from Orpiment. *And he :* Quicksilver of orpiment is Cambar of Magnesia, but quicksilver is sulphur ascending from the mixed* composite. Ye must, therefore, mix that thick thing with fiery venom, putrefy, and diligently pound until a spirit be produced, which is hidden in that other spirit ; then is made the tincture which is desired of you all.

The Forty-Fifth Dictum.

But PLATO *saith :* It behoves you all, O Masters, when those bodies are

---

* Some abbreviations in the printed editions obscure the passage. According to the second recension : " Sometimes it is Cambar and sometimes it is Orpiment, but here

being dissolved, to take care lest they be burnt up, as also to wash them with sea water, until all their salt be turned into sweetness, clarifies, tinges, becomes tincture of copper, and then goes off in flight ! Because it was necessary that one should become tingeing, and that the other should be tinged, for the spirit being separated from the body and hidden in the other spirit, both become volatile. Therefore the Wise have said that the gate of flight must not be opened for that which would flee, (or that which does not flee),* by whose flight death is occasioned, for by the conversion of the sulphureous thing into a spirit like unto itself, either becomes volatile, since they are made aeriform spirits prone to ascend in the air. But the Philosophers seeing that which was

---

it is needful to understand that Quicksilver Cambar is Magnesia," &c.

* The reading of the second recension is clearer, namely, " Close the door on the volatile, lest it take flight."

not volatile made volatile with the volatiles, iterated these to a body like to the non-volatiles, and put them into that from which they could not escape.* They iterated them to a body like unto the bodies from which they were extracted, and the same were then digested. But as for the statement of the Philosopher that the tingeing agent and that which is to be tinged are made one tincture, it refers to a spirit concealed in another humid spirit. Know also that one of the humid spirits is cold, but the other is hot, and although the cold humid is not adapted to the warm humid, nevertheless they are made one. Therefore, we prefer these two bodies, because by them we rule the whole work, namely, bodies by not-bodies, until incorporeals become bodies, steadfast in the fire, because they are

---

* In the second recension the passage reads thus: "Concerning these the Philosophers also said: They fled not with flying things, and yet were they made flying."

conjoined with volatiles, which is not possible in any body, these excepted. For spirits in every wise avoid bodies, but fugitives are restrained by incorporeals. Incorporeals, therefore, similarly flee from bodies; those, consequently, which do not flee are better and more precious than all bodies. These things, therefore, being done, take those which are not volatile and join them; wash the body with the incorporeal until the incorporeal receives a non-volatile body; convert the earth into water, water into fire, fire into air, and conceal the fire in the depths of the water, but the earth in the belly of the air, mingling the hot with the humid, and the cold with the dry. Know, also, that Nature overcomes Nature, Nature rejoices in Nature, Nature contains Nature.

The Forty-Sixth Dictum.

ATTAMUS *saith* : It is to be noted that the whole assembly of the Philosophers have frequently treated concerning

Rubigo.* Rubigo, however, is a fictitious and not a true name. *The* TURBA
answereth: Name, therefore, Rubigo by
its true name, for by this it is not
calumniated. *And he :* Rubigo is according to the work, because it is from gold
alone. *The* TURBA *answereth* : Why,
then, have the .Philosophers referred it
to the leech ? *He answereth :* Because
water is hidden in sulphureous gold as
the leech is in water ; rubigo, therefore, is rubefaction in the second work,
but to make rubigo is to whiten in the
former work, in which the Philosophers ordained that the flower of gold
should be taken and a proportion of
gold equally.

The Forty-Seventh Dictum.

MUNDUS *saith :* Thou hast already
treated sufficiently of Rubigo, O

---

* While this term properly signifies the rust or oxide
of metals, it was used in many senses by the alchemists,
for the redness of rust associated it in their idea with other
forms of red matter, and rust philosophical became a part
of the Great Mystery. The oxydes of iron, the oxydes of
lead, sulphate of mercury, sulphate of arsenic, sulphate of

Attamus! I will speak, therefore, of venom, and will instruct future generations that venom is not a body, because subtle spirits have made it into a tenuous spirit, have tinged the body and burned it with venom, which venom the Philosopher asserts will tinge every body. But the Ancient Philosophers thought that he who turned gold into venom had arrived at the purpose, but he who can do not this profiteth nothing. Now I say unto you, all ye Sons of the Doctrine, that unless ye reduce the thing by fire until those things ascend like a spirit, ye effect nought. This, therefore, is a spirit avoiding the fire and a ponderous smoke,* which when it enters the body

---

antimony, were all more or less confounded under the names of rubigo, minium, &c.

   * It is not, perhaps, surprising that what was above all things the mystery of the fire and the furnace, should concern itself considerably with the smoke in which it so often ended, and thus in various stages of its history we have alchemy discoursing of that specially philosophical smoke which is identical with scoriæ, and hence on the authority of the Greeks involves the whole art; we have also white smoke, identical with mercury; citrine smoke, identical

penetrates it entirely, and makes the body rejoice.* The Philosophers have all said: Take a black and conjoining spirit; therewith break up the bodies and torture them till they be altered.

The Forty-Eighth Dictum.

PYTHAGORAS *saith*: We must affirm unto all you seekers after this Art that the Philosophers have treated of conjunction (or continuation) in various ways. But I enjoin upon you to make quicksilver constrain the body of Magnesia, or the body Kuhul, or the Spume of Luna, or incombustible sulphur, or roasted calx, or alum which is out of apples, as ye know. But if there was any singular regimen for any of these, a Philosopher would not say so, as ye know. Understand,

---

with yellow sulphur; red smoke, which is orpiment; smoke of extreme subtlety, of which the Latin Geber discourses; and lastly the ponderous smoke of the *Turba.* Many others might be named, but these varieties are sufficient to show that smoke was as important to the alchemists as to the votaries of " my Lady Nicotine."

   * Otherwise : " the nature rejoices therein."

therefore, that sulphur, calx, and alum which is from apples, and Kuhul, are all nothing else but water of sulphur. Know ye also that Magnesia, being mixed with quicksilver and sulphur, they pursue one another. Hence you must not dismiss that Magnesia without the quicksilver, for when it is composed it is called an exceeding strong composition, which is one of the ten regimens established by the Philosophers. Know, also, that when Magnesia is whitened with quicksilver, you must congeal white water therein, but when it is reddened you must congeal red water, for, as the Philosophers have observed in their books, the regimen is not one.* Accordingly, the first congelation is of tin, copper, and lead. But the second is com-

---

* " There are other denominations," says Synesius in his letter to Dioscorus. " Thus whitening is a calcination, and yellowing an igneous regeneration; for some of these (substances) calcine themselves, and (other some) regenerate themselves. But the Philosopher has designated them under several names, and sometimes in the singular, sometimes in the plural person, in order to test us and see whether we are intelligent."

posed with water of sulphur.* Some, however, reading this book, think that the composition can be bought. It must be known for certain that nothing of the work can be bought, and that the science of this Art is nothing else than vapour and the sublimation of water, with the conjunction, also, of quicksilver in the body of Magnesia; † but, heretofore, the Philosophers have demonstrated in their books that the impure water of sulphur is from sulphur only, and no sulphur is produced without the water of its calx, and of quicksilver, and of sulphur.

The Forty-Ninth Dictum.

BELUS *saith* : O all ye Philosophers, ye have not dealt sparingly concerning composition and contact, but composition, contact, and congelation are one thing! Take, therefore, a part

---

* Or, "with sulphur and the water thereof."

† The second recension reads: "It is nothing but vapour and water, while the regimen is nothing but the sublimation of quicksilver and its union with the body of magnesia."

from the one composition and a part
out of ferment of gold,* and on these
impose pure water of sulphur.   This,
then, is the potent (or revealed) arcanum
which tinges every body.   PYTHAGORAS
answereth :   O Belus, why hast thou
called it a potent arcanum, yet hast
not shown its work ?   *And he* : In our
books, O Master, we have found
the same which thou hast received
from the ancients !   *And* PYTHAGORAS :
Therefore have I assembled you
together, that you might remove any
obscurities which are in any books.
And he : Willingly, O Master !   It is
to be noted that pure water which
is from sulphur is not composed of
sulphur alone, but is composed of
several things, for the one sulphur is
made out of several sulphurs.†   How,

---

* The ancient Latin treatise which passes as the work
of Morien, says sententiously : " The ferment of gold is
gold, even as the ferment of bread is bread." The statement is reproduced literally by the *Rosary of the Philosophers.*

† According to the second recension : "the clean
water which is from sulphur is not derived from sulphur

therefore, O Master, shall I compose these things that they may become one ? *And he :* Mix, O Belus, that which strives with the fire with that which does not strive, for things which are conjoined in a fire suitable to the same contend, because the warm venoms of the physician are cooked in a gentle, incomburent fire !* Surely ye perceive what the Philosophers have stated concerning decoction, that a little sulphur burns many strong things, and the humour which remains is called humid pitch, balsam of gum, and other like things. Therefore our Philosophers are made like to the physicians, notwithstanding that the tests of the physicians are more intense than those of the Philosophers. *The* TURBA *answereth :* I wish, O Belus, that you would also shew the disposition of this potent arcanum !

---

alone, but is composed of several things which make up one sulphur."

   * For this last sentence the second recension substitutes : "and friendship is made constant."

And he: I proclaim to future generations that this arcanum proceeds from
two compositions, that is to say,
sulphur and magnesia.   But after it
is reduced and conjoined into one,
the Philosophers have called it water,
spume of Boletus (*i.e.*, a species of
fungus), and the thickness of gold.
When, however, it has been reduced
into quicksilver, they call it sulphur
of water; sulphur also, when it contains sulphur, they term a fiery venom,
because it is a potent (or open) arcanum
which ascends from those things
ye know.

The Fiftieth Dictum.

PANDOLPHUS *saith* : If, O Belus, thou
dost describe the sublimation* of

---

* The Greek term which the alchemists of the
Byzantine collection made use of as the equivalent of sublimation, signified originally filings, as M. Berthelot informs
us, thus expressing the idea of the extreme attenuation of
matter.   The same idea was attached later on by the Latin
adepts to their term alcoolisation, "which signifies reduc-
tion to the condition of an impalpable powder. (*Collection
des Anciens Alchimistes Grecs*, Int., 210).   Another species
of sublimation was called *stalagma*, which meant distilla-
tion by vapourisation or filtration.   (*Ib.*, 211.)

sulphur for future generations, thou wilt accomplish an excellent thing! *And the* TURBA: Do thou show it forth, therefore, O Pandolphus! *And he*: The philosophers have ordered that quicksilver should be taken out of Cambar, and albeit they spoke truly, yet in these words there is a little ambiguity, the obscurity of which I will remove. See then that the quicksilver is sublimed in tabernacles, and extract the same from Cambar, but there is another Cambar in sulphur* which Belus hath demonstrated to you, for out of sulphur mixed with sulphur, many works proceed. When the same has been sublimed, there proceeds from the Cambar that quicksilver which is called Ethelia, Orpiment, Zendrio, or Sanderich,†

---

* According to the second recension: "there is another sulphur."

† The reading in the second recension is unintelligible. Sandarac is realgar; in the Greek MSS. it is confounded under the same sign as arsenic. M. Berthelot also tells us that it was confused anciently with minium and cinnabar, as indeed is quite plain from the Lexicon of Rulandus. The same authority reminds us that the name is applied at the present day to an entirely different composition, derived

Ebsemich, Magnesia, Kuhul, or Chuhul, and many other names. Concerning this, philosophers have said that, being ruled by its regimen (for ten is the perfection of all things), its white nature appears, nor is there any shadow therein. Then the envious* have called it lead from Ebmich, Magnesia, Marteck, White Copper. For, when truly whitened, it is devoid of shadow and blackness, it has left its thickened ponderous bodies, and therewith a clean humid spirit has ascended, which spirit is tincture. Accordingly, the wise have said that copper has a soul and a body. Now, its soul is spirit, and its body is thick. Therefore, it behoves you to destroy the thick body until ye extract a tingeing spirit from the same. Mix, also, the spirit extracted therefrom with light sulphur until you, investigators, find your design accomplished.

from colophon, and not known to the ancients under this designation.

* Throughout the second recension, " Philosophers " or " the Wise," are substituted for this term.

The Fifty-First Dictum.

HORFOLCOS* *saith :* Thou hast narrated nothing, O Pandolphus, save the last regimen of this body! Thou hast, therefore, composed an ambiguous description for readers. But if its regimen were commenced from the beginning, you would destroy this obscurity. *Saith the* TURBA : Speak, therefore, concerning this to posterity, so far as it may please you. *And he :* It behoves you, investigators of this Art, first to burn copper† in a gentle fire, like that required in the hatching of eggs. For it behoves you to burn it with its humidity lest its spirit be burnt, and let the vessel be closed on all sides, so that its colour [? heat] may be increased, the body of copper be destroyed, and its tingeing spirit be extracted,‡ concerning which the

---

* In the second recension the name is Morfoleus.

† Otherwise, " the humidity."

‡ According to the second recension : " when the fire is increased and the vessel sealed effectually, lest the body of the copper and its flying spirit be extracted."

envious have said : Take quicksilver out of the Flower of Copper, which also they have called the water of our copper, a fiery venom, and a substance extracted from all things, which further they have termed Ethelia, extracted out of many things.* Again, some have said that when all things become one, bodies are made not-bodies, but not-bodies bodies. And know, all ye investigators of this Art, that every body is dissolved with the spirit with which it is mixed, with which without doubt it becomes a similar spiritual thing, and that every spirit which has a tingeing colour of spirits, and is constant against fire, is altered and coloured by bodies. Blessed then be the name of Him who hath inspired the Wise with the idea of turning a body into a spirit having strength and colour, unalterable and incorruptible, so that what formerly was volatile sulphur is now made sulphur not-volatile,

---

* Otherwise : "which flower of copper they have called our water, and fiery venom extracted from iron."

and incombustible! Know, also, all ye sons of learning, that he who is able to make your fugitive spirit red by the body mixed with it, and then from that body and that spirit can extract the tenuous nature hidden in the belly thereof, by a most subtle regimen, tinges every body, if only he is patient in spite of the tedium of extracting. Wherefore the envious have said: Know that out of copper, after it is humectated by the moisture thereof, is pounded in its water, and is cooked in sulphur, if ye extract a body having Ethelia, ye will find that which is suitable as a tincture for anything. Wherefore the envious have said: Things that are diligently pounded in the fire, with sublimation of the Ethelia, become fixed tinctures. For whatsoever words ye find in any man's book signify quicksilver, which we call water of sulphur,* which also

---

* Water of sulphur occurs among the ingredients of a recipe cited from Mary in one of the treatises of Zosimus, and in the *Detailed Exposition of the Work*, the following

we sometimes say is lead and copper and copulated coin.

The Fifty-Second Dictum.

IXUMDRUS *saith :* You will have treated most excellently, O Horfolcus, concerning the regimen of copper and the humid spirit, provided you proceed therewith. *And he :* Perfect, therefore, what I have omitted, O Ixumdrus! IXUMDRUS *saith :* You must know that this Ethelia* which you have previously mentioned and notified, which also the envious have called by many names, doth whiten, and tinge when it is whitened; then truly the Philosophers have called it the Flower of Gold, because it is a certain natural thing.

---

process occurs: "Water of sulphur obtained by means of calx is manfactured in this manner: Having mixed all the waters in the catalogue (which it is impossible to extricate from its context and place in the compass of a footnote), taking equal parts, add white earths until the compound becomes very white. Place in a mortar, kindle a fire underneath, and receive what distils." There is also a "pure" water of sulphur which is obtained somewhat differently.

* The second recension reads: "Water of Ethelia."

Do you not remember what the Philosophers have said, that before it arrives at this terminus, copper does not tinge ?* But when it is tinged it tinges, because quicksilver tinges when it is combined with its tincture. But when it is mixed with those ten things which the Philosophers have denominated fermented urines, then have they called all these things Multiplication. But some have termed their mixed bodies Corsufle and Gum of Gold.† Therefore, those names which are found in the books of the Philo-

---

* According to the second recension : " Before it reaches this point, it is called copper."

† That is to say, the Chrysocorallos of the Greek alchemists. The following is from a ricipe of Pseudo-Democritus : " Minera of Silver, 1 part ; Finest Earth of Chios, or Ochre, 2 parts ; Minium of Pontus, 1 part ; preparation given previously (it is too complicated for reproduction here), 2 parts : combine with the humour of the Sulphur (another abstruse recipe) ; cook over a fire carefully regulated. You will find a potent substance, having the colour of cinnabar, coral, or minium. This great wonder, this indescribable marvel, is called Chrysocorallos (Coral of Gold)." And Synesius, quoting Democritus, says : " Here is how he expresses himself: The body (metal) of magnesia, alone (produces) Chrysocoral."

sophers, and are thought superfluous and vain, are true and yet are fictitious, because they are one thing, one opinion, and one way. This is the quicksilver which is indeed extracted from all things,* out of which all things are produced, which also is pure water that destroys the shade of copper.   And know ye that this quicksilver, when it is whitened, becomes a sulphur which contains sulphur, and is a venom that has a brilliance like marble ; this the envious call Ethelia, orpiment and sandarac, out of which a tincture and pure spirit ascends with a mild fire, and the whole pure flower is sublimated, which flower becomes wholly quicksilver.   It is, therefore, a most great arcanum which the Philosophers have thus described, because sulphur alone whitens copper.   Ye, O investigators of this Art, must know that the said sulphur cannot whiten

---

* The reading *ab hominibus* for *ab omnibus* is substituted by the second recension several times in this Dictum, but there can be no doubt that it is a printer's error.

copper until it is whitened in the work!
And know ye also that it is the habit
of this sulphur to escape. When,
therefore, it flees from its own thick
bodies, and is sublimated as a vapour,
then it behoves you to retain it otherwise with quicksilver of its own kind,
lest it vanish altogether. Wherefore
the Philosophers have said, that
sulphurs are contained by sulphurs.
Know, further, that sulphurs tinge, and
then are they certain to escape unless
they are united to quicksilver of its
own kind. Do not, therefore, think
that because it tinges* and afterwards
escapes, it is the coin of the Vulgar, for
what the Philosophers are seeking is
the coin of the Philosophers, which,
unless it be mixed with white or red,
which is quicksilver of its own kind,
would doubtless escape. I direct you,
therefore, to mix quicksilver with quicksilver (of its kind) until together they
become one clean water composed out

---

* The second recension substitutes "fixes bodies,"
but both readings are obscure and seemingly corrupt.

of two. This is, therefore, the great arcanum, the confection of which is with its own gum; it is cooked with flowers in a gentle fire and with earth; it is made red with mucra and with vinegar, salt, and nitre,* and with mutal is turned into rubigo, or by any of the select tingeing agents existing in our coin.

The Fifty-Third Dictum.

EXUMENUS† *saith:* The envious have laid waste the whole Art with the multiplicity of names, but the entire work must be the Art of the Coin. For the Philosophers have ordered the doctors of this art to make coin-like gold, which also the same Philosophers have called by all manner of names. *The* TURBA *answereth:* Inform, therefore, posterity, O Exumenus, concern-

---

* M. Berthelot explains that the substance referred to under the terms Nitrum and Natron was really Carbonate of Soda, and that Nitre or Saltpetre was scarcely known in antiquity, nor, indeed, till the 6th century.

† For this name the second recension substitutes Obsemeganus.

ing a few of these names, that they may take warning ! *And he :* They have named it salting, sublimating, washing, and pounding Ethelias, whitening in the fire, frequently cooking vapour and coagulating, turning into rubigo, the confection of Ethel, the art of the water of sulphur and coagula. By all these names is that operation called which has pounded and whitened copper. And know ye, that quicksilver is white to the sight, but when it is possessed by the smoke of sulphur, it reddens and becomes Cambar. Therefore, when quicksilver is cooked with its confections it is turned into red, and hence the Philosopher saith that the nature of lead is swiftly converted. Do you not see that the Philosophers have spoken without envy ? Hence we deal in many ways with pounding and reiteration, that ye may extract the spirits existing in the vessel, which the fire did not cease to burn continuously. But the

M

water placed with those things prevents the fire from burning, and it befalls those things that the more they are possessed by the flame of fire, the more they are hidden in the depths of the water, lest they should be injured by the heat of the fire; but the water receives them in its belly and repels the flame of fire from them. *The* TURBA *answereth:* Unless ye make bodies not-bodies ye achieve nothing. But concerning the sublimation of water the Philosophers have treated not a little. And know that unless ye diligently pound the thing in the fire, the Ethelia does not ascend, but when that does not ascend ye achieve nothing. When, however, it ascends it is an instrument for the intended tincture with which ye tinge, and concerning this Ethelia HERMES saith: Sift the things which ye know; but another: Liquefy the things. Therefore, Arras saith: Unless ye pound the thing diligently in the fire, Ethelia does not ascend. The Master hath put forth a view which I shall now explain to the reasoners. Know ye that a very great wind of the south, when it is stirred up, sublimates clouds and elevates the vapours of the sea. *The* TURBA *answereth:* Thou hast dealt obscurely. *And he:* I will explain the testa,* and the vessel wherein is incombustible sulphur. But I order you to congeal fluxible quicksilver out of many things, that two may be made three, and four one, and two one.

The Fifty-Fourth Dictum.

ANAXAGORAS *saith:* Take the volatile burnt thing which lacks a body, and incorporate it. Then take the ponderous thing, having smoke, and thirsting

---

* Two meanings are given to this term in the *Lexicon of Rulandus.* The first is Bloom, Flower, &c., understood metallurgically; the second is a vessel of baked clay. Paracelsus uses it in an arbitrary fashion of his own to signify the skin of man's body. Compare the red Adamic earth or clay; it is probably a variation of the same idea.

to imbibe. *The* TURBA *answereth :*
Explain, O Anaxagoras, what is this
obscurity which you expound, and
beware of being envious ! *And he :* I
testify to you that this volatile burnt
thing, and this other which thirsts, are
Ethelia, which has been conjoined
with sulphur. Therefore, place these
in a glass vessel over the fire, and
cook until the whole becomes Cambar.
Then God will accomplish the arcanum
ye seek. But I direct you to cook
continuously, and not to grow tired of
repeating the process. And know ye
that the perfection of this work is
the confection of water of sulphur
with tabula ;* finally, it is cooked
until it becomes Rubigo, for all the
Philosophers have said : He who is
able to turn Rubigo into golden
venom has already achieved the desired work, but otherwise his labour
is vain.

---

* According to the second recension : " The whole
perfection of sulphur consists in the decoction of
tabula."

The Fifty-Fifth Dictum.

ZENON* *saith :* Pythagoras hath treated concerning the water, which the envious have called by all names. Finally, at the end of his book he has treated of the ferment of gold, ordaining that thereon should be imposed clean water of sulphur, and a small quantity of its gum. I am astonished, O all ye Turba, how the envious have in this work discoursed of the perfection rather than the commencement of the same! *The* TURBA *answereth :* Why, therefore, have you left it to putrefy? *And he :* Thou hast spoken truly ; putrefaction does not take place without the dry and the humid. But the vulgar putrefy with the humid. Thus the humid is merely coagulated with the dry. But out of both is the beginning of the work. Notwithstanding, the envious have divided this work into three parts, asserting that one quickly flees, but the other is fixed and immovable.

---

* The name in the second recension is Pitheon.

The Fifty-Sixth Dictum.

CONSTANS *saith:* What have you to do with the treatises of the envious, for it is necessary that this work should deal with four things? *They answer:* Demonstrate, therefore, what are those four? *And he:* Earth, water, air, and fire. Ye have then those four elements without which nothing is ever generated, nor is anything absolved in the Art. Mix, therefore, the dry with the humid, which are earth and water, and cook in the fire and in the air, whence the spirit and the soul are dessicated.* And know ye that the tenuous tingeing agent takes its power out of the tenuous part of the earth, out of the tenuous part of the fire and of the air, while out of the tenuous part of the water, a tenuous spirit has been dessicated.† This, therefore, is the process of our work,

---

* According to the second recension: " The spirit is dessiccated in the soul."

† The second recension merely says that the power in question is derived from the tenuous part of the earth, air, and water.

namely, that everything may be turned into earth when the tenuous parts of these things are extracted, because a body is then composed which is a kind of atmospheric thing, and thereafter tinges the imposed body of coins.* Beware, however, O all ye investigators of this art, lest ye multiply things, for the envious have multiplied and destroyed for you! They have also described various regimens that they might deceive; they have further called it (or have likened it to) the humid with all the humid, and the dry with all the dry, by the name of every stone and metal, gall of animals of the sea, the winged things of heaven and reptiles of the earth. But do ye who would tinge observe that bodies are tinged with bodies. For I say to you what the Philosopher said briefly and truly at the beginning of his book. In the art of gold is the quicksilver from Cambar, and in coins

---

* The reading of the second recension has been partly substituted in this unintelligible passage.

is the quicksilver from the Male. In
nothing, however, look beyond this,
since the two quicksilvers are also
one.

The Fifty-Seventh Dictum.

ACRATUS* *saith:* I signify to posterity
that I make philosophy near to the
Sun and Moon. He, therefore, that
will attain to the truth let him take
the moisture of the Sun and the
Spume† of the Moon.‡ *The* TURBA
answereth: Why are you made an
adversary to your brethren? *And he:*
I have spoken nothing but the truth.
But they: Take what the Turba hath
taken. *And he:* I was so intending,
yet, if you are willing, I direct posterity to take a part of the coins
which the Philosophers have ordered,
which also Hermes has adapted to

---

* In the second recension the name is Astratus.

† Otherwise the spirit; it is probably a misreading.

‡ This one of the two passages which seem to indicate
any planetary attribution of the metals, but even here it may
be an analogy borrowed from the astronomy of the period
without any real attribution. The distinction between
mercury and quicksilver in the 67th Dictum should be
noted.

the true tingeing,* and a part of the copper of the Philosophers, to mix the same with the coins, and place all the four bodies in the vessel, the mouth of which must be carefully closed, lest the water escape. Cooking must proceed for seven days, when the copper, already pounded with the coins, is found turned into water. Let both be again slowly cooked, and fear nothing. Then let the vessel be opened, and a blackness will appear above. Repeat the process, cook continually until the blackness of Kuhul, which is from the blackness of coins, be consumed. For when that is consumed a precious whiteness will appear on them; finally, being returned to their place, they are cooked until the whole is dried and is turned into stone. Also repeatedly and continuously cook that stone born of copper and coins with a fire

---

* According to the second recension: "take a part of the coins of the Philosophers, which are the coins of Hermes."

sharper than the former, until the stone is destroyed, broken up, and turned into cinder, which is a precious cinder. Alas, O ye sons of the Doctrine, how precious is that which is produced from it! Mixing, therefore, the cinder with water, cook again, until that cinder liquefy therewith, and then cook and imbue with permanent water, until the composition becomes sweet and mild and red. Imbue until it becomes humid. Cook in a still hotter fire, and carefully close the mouth of the vessel, for by this regimen fugitive bodies become not-fugitive, spirits are turned into bodies, bodies into spirits, and both are connected together. Then are spirits made bodies having a tingeing and germinating soul. *The* TURBA *answereth:* Now hast thou notified to posterity that Rubigo attaches itself to copper after the blackness is washed off with permanent water. Then it is congealed and becomes a body of magnesia. Finally, it is cooked until the whole body is broken up. Afterwards the volatile is turned into a cinder and becomes copper without its shadow. Attrition also truly takes place. Concerning, therefore, the work of the Philosophers, what hast thou delivered to posterity, seeing that thou hast by no means called things by their proper names? *And he* : Following your own footsteps, I have discoursed even as have you. BONELLUS *answereth* : You speak truly, for if you did otherwise we should not order your sayings to be written in our books.

The Fifty-Eighth Dictum.

BALGUS* *saith* : The whole Turba, O Acratus, has already spoken, as you have seen, but a benefactor sometimes deceives, though his intention is to do good. *And they:* Thou speakest truly. Proceed, therefore, according to thy opinion, and beware of envy! *Then he:*

---

* In the second recension this speech is put into the mouth of Anastratus.

You must know that the envious have described this arcanum in the shade ; in physical reasoning and astronomy, and the art of images ; they have also likened it to trees ; they have ambiguously concealed it by the names of metals, vapours, and reptiles ; as is generally perceived in all their work. I, nevertheless, direct you, investigators of this science, to take iron and draw it into plates ; finally, mix (or sprinkle) it with venom, and place it in its vessel, the mouth of which must be closed most carefully, and beware lest ye too much increase the humour, or, on the other hand, lest it be too dry, but stir it vigorously as a mass, because, if the water be in excess, it will not be contained in the chimney, while, if it be too dry, it will neither be conjoined nor cooked in the chimney ; hence I direct you to confect it diligently ; finally, place it in its vessel, the mouth of which must be closed internally and externally with clay, and, having kindled coals above it, after some days ye shall open it, and there shall ye find the iron plates already liquefied; while on the lid of the vessel ye shall find globules. For when the fire is kindled the vinegar* ascends, because its spiritual nature passes into the air, wherefore, I direct you to keep that part separately. Ye must also know that by multiplied† decoctions and attritions it is congealed and coloured by the fire, and its nature is changed. By a similar decoction and liquefaction Cambar is not disjoined.‡ I notify to you that

---

* Among the Greek technical treatises there is one entitled *The Work of the Four Elements,* and this contains a brief section on the *Nomenclature of the Divine Vinegar and the Divine Water,* which is worth citing in connection with the question of the unity of subjects amidst the multiplicity of names. Here is what the Philosophers say on this subject : " Divine water, divine vinegar, white magnesia, water of calx, virgin's urine, mercury, sea water, virginal milk, milk of the she ass, the bitch, the black cow, alum water, ash of cabbage, of natron, occidental matter, vapour. There is the substance which whitens the body of magnesia, that is, burnt copper, &c."

† The number three is indicated by the second recension.

‡ The second recension says that it *is* disjoined.

by the said frequent decoction the weight of a third part of the water is consumed, but the residue becomes a wind in the Cambar of the second spirit.* And know ye that nothing is more precious or more excellent than the red sand of the sea, for the Sputum of Luna is united with the light of the Sun's rays.† Luna is perfected by the coming on of night, and by the heat of the Sun the dew is congealed. Then, that being wounded, the dew of the death-dealer is joined,‡ and the more the days pass on the more intensely is it congealed, and is not burned. For he who cooks with the Sun is himself congealed,§ and that signal whiteness causes it to overcome the terrene fire.

---

* "Which Cambar and its spirit bears in the belly thereof," is the alternative reading.

† According to the second recension, the sand is "the spume of the Moon, which is joined to the light of the Sun, and is congealed."

‡ Omitted in the second recension.

§ For this nonsensical passage the second recension substitutes: "That which is cooked by the heat of the Sun is congealed."

Then saith BONITES: Do you not know,
O Balgus, that the Spume of Luna
tinges nothing except our copper?
And BALGUS: Thou speakest truly.
And he: Why, therefore, hast thou
omitted to describe that tree, of the fruit
whereof whosoever eateth shall hunger
nevermore? *And* BALGUS: A certain
person,* who has followed science, has
notified to me after what manner he
discovered this same tree, and appro-
priately operating, did extract the
fruit and eat of it. But when I
inquired of him concerning the growth
and the increment, he described that
pure whiteness, thinking that the same
is found without any laborious disposition. Then its perfection is the fruit
thereof. But when I further asked
how it is nourished with food until it
fructifies, he said: Take that tree, and
build a house about it, which shall
wholly surround the same, which shall
also be circular, dark, encircled by

---

* In the second recension this person is referred to
as Tulleas.

dew, and shall have placed on it a
man of a hundred years; shut and
secure the door lest dust or wind should
reach them. Then in the time of 180
days send them away to their homes.
I say that man shall not cease to eat
of the fruit of that tree to the perfection of the number [of the days] until
the old man shall become young. O
what marvellous natures, which have
transformed the soul of that old man
into a juvenile body, and the father is
made into the son! Blessed be thou,
O most excellent God!

The Fifty-Ninth Dictum.

THEOPHILUS *saith:* I propose to speak
further concerning those things which
Bonites hath narrated. *And the*
TURBA: Speak, Brother, for thy
brother hath discoursed elegantly.
And he: Following in the steps of
Bonites I will make perfect his say-
ings. It should be known that all the
Philosophers, while they have con-
cealed this disposition, yet spoke the

truth in their treatises when they named water of life, for this reason, that whatsoever* is mixed with the said water first dies, then lives and becomes young. And know, all ye disciples, that iron does not become rusty except by reason of this water, because it tinges the plates ; it is then placed in the sun till it liquefies and is imbued, after which it is congealed. In these days it becomes rusty, but silence is better than this illumination. *The* TURBA *answereth :* O Theophilus, beware of becoming envious, and complete thy speech ! *And he :* Would that I might repeat the like thing ! *And they :* What is thy will ? *Then he :* Certain fruits, which proceed first from that perfect tree, do flourish in the beginning of the summer, and the more they are multiplied the more are they adorned,† until they are

---

* The reference in the second recension is to the old man of the previous dictum.

† According to the second recension : " The more the tree is adorned."

N

perfected, and being mature become sweet. In the same way that woman,* fleeing from her own children, with whom she lives, although partly angry, yet does not brook being overcome, nor that her husband should possess her beauty, who furiously loves her, and keeps awake contending with her, till he shall have carnal intercourse with her, and God make perfect the fœtus, when he multiplies children to himself according to his pleasure. His beauty, therefore, is consumed by fire who does not approach his wife except by reason of lust. For when the term is finished he turns to her. I also make known to you that the dragon never dies, but the Philosophers have put to death the woman who slays her spouses. For the belly of that

---

* The compiler of the *Turba* seems to have introduced this allegory from another source, or it has possibly been interpolated at a later period ; its style, indeed, is that of the epoch of Trevisan ; it is, in any case, quite out of character with the text as a whole, and refers, it will be seen, to something which has not been previously described.

woman is full of weapons and venom. Let, therefore, a sepulchre be dug for the dragon, and let that woman be buried with him, who being strongly joined with that woman, the more he clasps her and is entwined with her, the more his body, by the creation of female weapons in the body of the woman, is cut up into parts. For perceiving him mixed with the limbs of a woman he becomes secure from death, and the whole is turned into blood. But the Philosophers, beholding him turned into blood, leave him in the sun for certain days, until the lenitude is consumed, the blood dries up, and they find that venom which now is manifest. Then the wind is hidden.

The Sixtieth Dictum.

BONELLUS* *saith:* Know, all ye disciples, that out of the elect things nothing becomes useful without con-

---

* In the second recension the name is Bodillus.

junction and regimen,* because sperma
is generated out of blood and desire.
For the man mingling with the woman,
the sperm is nourished by the humour
of the womb, and by the moistening
blood, and by heat, and when forty
nights have elapsed the sperm is
formed. But if the humidity of the
blood and of the womb were not heat,
the sperm would not be dissolved, nor
the fœtus be procreated. But God
has constituted that heat and blood
for the nourishment of the sperm until
the fœtus is brought forth, after which
it is not nourished, save by milk and
fire, sparingly and gradually, while it
is dust, and the more it burns the
more, the bones being strengthened,
it is led towards youth, arriving
at which it is independent.† Thus
it behoves you also to act in

---

* Otherwise: "Know that nothing is generated
without complexion."

† This absurd confusion is not found in the second
recension, which reads: "So long as it is little, it is
nourished with milk, and in proportion as the vital heat
is maintained, the bones are strengthened."

this Art. Know ye that without heat nothing is ever generated, and that the bath causes the matter to perish by means of intense heat. If, indeed, it be frigid, it puts to flight and disperses, but if it have been tempered, it is con-venient and sweet to the body, where-fore the veins become smooth and the flesh is augmented. Behold it has been demonstrated to you, all ye disciples! Understand, therefore, and in all things which ye attempt to rule, fear God.

The Sixty-First Dictum.

MOSES *saith :* It is to be observed that the envious have named lead of copper instruments of formation, simulating, deceiving prosterity,* to whom I give notice that there are no instruments except from our own white, strong, and splendid powder, and from our

---

* This passage is so corrupt as to be almost un-translatable. According to the second recension: "The envious have in many ways described the process of making lead, and have represented that there are a number of instruments," etc.

concave stone* and marble, to the
whole work whereof there is no more
suitable powder, nor one more conjoined to our composition, than the
powder of Alociæ,† out of which are
produced instruments of formation.
Further, the Philosophers have already
said : Take instruments out of the egg.
Yet they have not said what the egg
is, nor of what bird.‡   And know ye

---

* The concave stone does not seem to be a term
which entered into the nomenclature of later philosophers.
We hear much concerning the form of the stone, but that
is not to be understood as its configuration, being used in
the same sense as Latin theology was accustomed to speak of
the form of the soul. So Bernard Trevisan, in his *Epistle to
Thomas of Bononia:* "Our stone does not possess a
formal form (*forma formabilis*) such as vegetative or
sensitive, yet, nevertheless, it has a formed form (*forma
formata*), which form is the elements themselves, and this
is because it is homogeneous, whereas the human body,
or that of other sensitive things, is heterogeneous." For
the term concave stone the second recension substitutes
gleaming, *i.e., candidus.*

† A severe critic, having failed to trace this term,
might suggest a slight emendation, and read *Alogiæ,*
i.e., " many words and no sense."

‡ This entire passage is considerably shortened in the
second recension, which simply observes that out of the
powder mentioned at the beginning, instruments adapted
to the egg are composed, but that at the same time the
envious have omitted to name the egg, etc.

that the regimen of these things is more difficult than the entire work, because, if the composition be ruled more than it should be, its light is taken and extinguished by the sea. Wherefore the Philosophers have ordered that it should be ruled with profound judgment. The moon, therefore, being at the full, take this and place in sand till it be dissolved. And know ye that while ye are placing the same in sand and repeating the process, unless ye have patience, ye err in ruling, and corrupt the work. Cook, therefore, the same in a gentle fire until ye see that it is dissolved. Then extinguish with vinegar, and ye shall find one thing separated from three companions. And know ye that the first, Ixir, commingles, the second burns, while the third liquefies.* In

---

* Alchemy does not seem to have generally recognised the existence of three elixirs. Fundamentally, indeed, it holds there is but one elixir, having various degrees of perfection. Zosimus, however, recognises in the true powder of perfection the existence of three powers and three activities proceeding from those powers, namely,

the first place, therefore, impose nine ounces of vinegar twice—first while the vessel is being made hot, and second when it is heated.

The Sixty-Second Dictum.

MUNDUS *saith :* It behoves you, O all ye seekers after this Art, to know that whatsoever the Philosophers have narrated or ordained, Kenckel, herbs, geldum, and carmen, are one thing !* Do not, therefore, trouble about a plurality of things, for there is one Tyrian tincture of the Philosophers to which they have given names at will, and having abolished the proper name, they have called it black, because it has been extracted from our sea. And

---

tincture, penetration, and fixation, just as a body has mathematically three dimensions. The distinction is a mere subtlety. Later alchemists speak much of the Elixir at the White and the Elixir at the Red, yet the second is the first in exaltation, and so also the Elixir of metals is at the same time held to be the medicine of men.

* According to the second recension : '' Certain Philosophers have named Gold Chelidony, Karnech, Geldum, etc.''

know that the ancient priests did
not condescend to wear artificial
garments, whence, for purifying altars,
and lest they should introduce into
them anything sordid or impure, they
tinged Kenckel with a Tyrian colour;
but our Tyrian colour, which they
placed in their altars and treasuries,
was more clean and fragrant than
can be described by me, which also
has been extracted from our red
and most pure sea, which is sweet and
of a pleasant odour, and is neither
sordid nor impure in putrefaction.
And know ye that we have given
many names to it, which are all
true—an example of which, for those
that possess understanding, is to be
traced in corn that is being ground.
For after grinding it is called by
another name, and after it has been
passed through the sieve, and the
various substances have been separated one from another, each of these
has its own name, and yet fundamentally there is but one name, to

wit, corn, from which many names are distinguished. Thus we call the purple in each grade of its regimen by the name of its own colour.

The Sixty-Third Dictum.

PHILOSOPHUS* *saith :* I notify to posterity that the nature is male and female, wherefore the envious have called it the body of Magnesia, because therein is the most great arcanum ! Accordingly, O all ye seekers after this Art, place Magnesia in its vessel, and cook diligently ! Then, opening it after some days, ye shall find the whole changed into water. Cook further until it be coagulated, and contain itself. But, when ye hear of the sea in the books of the envious, know that they signify humour, while by the basket they signify the vessel, and by the medicines they mean Nature, because it germinates

* In the second recension, this speech is put into the mouth of Rarson.

and flowers.* But when the envious
say : Wash until the blackness of the
copper passes away, certain people name
this blackness coins. But Agadimon
has clearly demonstrated when he
boldly put forth these words : It is to
be noted, O all ye demonstrators of
this art, that the things [or the copper]
being first mixed and cooked once, ye
shall find the prescribed blackness!
That is to say, they all become black.
This, therefore, is the lead of the
Wise, concerning which they have
treated very frequently in their books.
Some also call it [the lead] of our
black coins.

The Sixty-Fourth Dictum.†

PYTHAGORAS *saith :* How marvellous
is the diversity of the Philosophers
in those things which they formerly
asserted, and in their coming together [or agreement], in respect

---

* According to the second recension : "That which
buds and flowers is one nevertheless."

† This dictum is omitted altogether by the second
recension.

of this small and most common thing, wherein the precious thing is concealed! And if the vulgar knew, O all ye investigators of this art, the same small and vile thing, they would deem it a lie! Yet, if they knew its efficacy, they would not vilify it, but God hath concealed this from the crowd* lest the world should be devastated.

The Sixty-Fifth Dictum.

HORFOLCUS *saith* :† You must know, O all ye who love wisdom, that whereas Mundus hath been teaching this Art, and placing before you most lucid syllogisms, he that does not understand what he has said is a brute animal! But I will explain the regimen of this small thing, in order that any one, being introduced into this Art, may become bolder,‡

---

* Literally "from the sea."

† In the second recension the speaker is called Orfulus.

‡ On the principle of Zosimus: "Be not dissuaded by thine inexperience, and when you perceive that everything has become ash, understand then that all goes well."—*On the Diversity of Burnt Copper.*

may more assuredly consider it, and although it be small, may compose the common with that which is dear, and the dear with that which is common. Know ye that in the beginning of the mixing, it behoves you to commingle elements which are crude, gentle, sincere, and not cooked or governed, over a gentle fire. Beware of intensifying the fire until the elements are conjoined, for these should follow one another, and be embraced in a complexion, whereby they are gradually burnt, until they be dessicated in the said gentle fire. And know that one spirit burns one thing and destroys one thing, and one body strengthens one spirit, and teaches the same to contend with the fire. But, after the first combustion, it is necessary that it should be washed, cleansed, and dealbated on the fire until all things become one colour; with which, afterwards, it behoves you to mix the residuum of the whole humour, and then its colour will be exalted. For the elements, being diligently cooked in the fire, rejoice, and are changed into different natures, because the liquefied, which is the lead, becomes not-liquefied,* the humid becomes dry, the thick body becomes a spirit, and the fleeing spirit becomes strong and fit to do battle against the fire. Whence the Philosopher saith: Convert the elements and thou shalt find what thou seekest. But to convert the elements is to make the moist dry and the fugitive fixed. These things being accomplished by the disposition, let the operator leave it in the fire until the gross be made subtle, and the subtle remain as a tingeing spirit. Know ye, also, that the death and life of the elements proceed from fire, and that the composite germinates itself, and produces that which ye desire, God favouring. But when the colours begin ye shall behold the miracles of the wisdom

---

* According to the second recension: " The non-liquid becomes liquid which is the head of this art."

of God, until the Tyrian colour be accomplished. O wonder-working Nature, tingeing other natures! O heavenly Nature, separating and converting the elements by regimen! Nothing, therefore, is more precious than these Natures in that Nature which multiplies the composite, and makes fixed and scarlet.

The Sixty-Sixth Dictum.*

EXEMIGANUS *saith:* Thou hast already treated, O Lucas, concerning living and concealed silver, which is Magnesia, as it behoves thee, and thou hast commanded posterity to prove [or to experiment] and to read the books, knowing what the Philosophers have said: Search the latent spirit and disesteem it not, seeing that when it remains it is a great arcanum and effects many good things.

---

* This dictum is omitted in the second recension, and that which follows is put into the mouth of Emiganus.

The Sixty-Seventh Dictum.

LUCAS *saith*: I testify to posterity, and what I set forth is more lucid than are your words, that the Philosopher saith:* Burn the copper, burn the silver, burn the gold. HERMIGANUS *replies*: Behold something more dark than ever! *The* TURBA *answereth*: Illumine, therefore, that which is dark. *And he*: As to that which he said—Burn, burn, burn, the diversity is only in the names, for they are one and the same thing. *And they*: Woe unto you! how shortly hast thou dealt with it! why art thou poisoned with jealousy! *And he*: Is it desirable that I should speak more clearly? *And they*: Do so. *And he*: I signify that to whiten is to burn, but to make red is life.† For the envious have

---

* The following variation occurs in the opening of the second recension: " The books of the Philosophers should be read, for they have not in vain advised that the sucking child should be heeded, for therein is an arcanum, out of which the Wise have operated good things."

† According to the second recension: " To make red is to vivify."

multiplied many names that they
might lead posterity astray, to whom
I testify that the definition of this Art
is the liquefaction of the body and
the separation of the soul from the
body, seeing that copper, like a man,
has a soul and a body. Therefore,
it behoves you, O all ye Sons of the
Doctrine, to destroy the body and
extract the soul therefrom! Wherefore the Philosophers said that the
body does not penetrate the body,
but that there is a subtle nature,
which is the soul, and it is this which
tinges and penetrates the body. In
nature, therefore, there is a body
and there is a soul. *The* TURBA
answereth: Despite your desire to
explain, you have put forth dark
words. *And he:* I signify that the
envious have narrated and said that
the splendour of Saturn does not
appear unless it perchance be dark
when it ascends in the air, that
Mercury is hidden by the rays of the
Sun, that quicksilver vivifies the body

o

by its fiery strength, and thus the work is accomplished. But Venus, when she becomes oriental, precedes the Sun.*

The Sixty-Eighth Dictum.

ATTAMUS *saith:* Know, O all ye investigators of this Art, that our work, of which ye have been inquiring, is produced by the generation of the sea, by which and with which, after God, the work is completed! Take, therefore, Halsut and old sea stones, and boil with coals until they become white. Then extinguish in white vinegar. If 24 ounces thereof have been boiled, let the heat be extinguished with a third part of the vinegar, that is, 8 ounces; pound with white vinegar, and cook in the sun and black earth for 42 days. But the second work is performed from the tenth day of the month of September to the tenth day

---

* This is the second of the two passages mentioned in the note on page 168 of this volume as containing traces of a planetary attribution of metals, but, as in the 57th Dictum, the reference may be astronomical and not chemical.

[or grade] of Libra. Do not impose the vinegar a second time in this work, but leave the same to be cooked until all its vinegar be dried up and it becomes a fixed earth, like Egyptian earth. And the fact that one work is congealed more quickly and another more slowly, arises from the diversity of cooking. But if the place where it is cooked be humid and dewy it is congealed more quickly, while if it be dry it is congealed more slowly.

The Sixty-Ninth Dictum.

FLORUS *saith:* I am thinking of perfecting thy treatise, O Mundus, for thou has not accomplished the disposition of the cooking! *And he:* Proceed, O Philosopher! *And* FLORUS: I teach you, O Sons of the Doctrine, that the sign of the goodness of the first decoction is the extraction of its redness! *And he:* Describe what is redness. *And* FLORUS: When ye see that the matter is entirely black, know that

whiteness has been hidden in the
belly of that blackness. Then it behoves you to extract that whiteness
most subtly from that blackness, for
ye know how to discern between them.
But in the second decoction let that
whiteness be placed in a vessel with
its instruments, and let it be cooked
gently until it become completely
white. But when, O all ye seekers
after this Art, ye shall perceive that
whiteness appear and flowing over all,
be certain that redness is hid in that
whiteness! However, it does not
behove you to extract it,* but rather
to cook it until the whole become a
most deep red, with which nothing
can compare. Know also that the
first blackness is produced out of the
nature of Marteck, and that redness
is extracted from that blackness,
which red has improved the black,
and has made peace between the
fugitive and the non-fugitive, reducing

---

* The second recension affirms that it does behove
you to extract it.

the two into one. *The* TURBA *answereth:* And why was this? *And he:* Because the cruciated matter when it is submerged in the body, changes it into an unalterable and indelible nature. It behoves you, therefore, to know this sulphur which blackens the body. And know ye that the same sulphur cannot be handled, but it cruciates and tinges. And the sulphur which blackens is that which does not open the door to the fugitive and turns into the fugitive with the fugitive.* Do you not see that the cruciating does not cruciate with harm or corruption, but by coadunation and utility of things?† For if its victim were noxious and inconvenient, it would not be embraced thereby until its colours were extracted from it unalterable and

---

* According to the second recension: "It converts that which is non-fugitive into a fugitive nature." Both readings are corrupt and ungrammatical.

† The second recension somewhat reverses this, reading: "That which cruciates with harm or corruption does not cruciate with utility and coadunation."

indelible. This we have called water of sulphur, which water we have prepared for the red tinctures; for the rest it does not blacken; but that which does blacken, and this does not come to pass without blackness, I have testified to be the key of the work.

The Seventieth Dictum.

MUNDUS* *saith* : Know, all ye investigators of this Art, that the head is all things, which if it hath not, all that it imposes profits nothing. Accordingly, the Masters have said that what is perfected is one, and a diversity of natures does not improve that thing, but one and a suitable nature, which it behoves you to rule carefully, for by ignorance of ruling some have erred. Do not heed, therefore, the plurality of these compositions, nor those things which the philosophers have enumerated in their books. For the nature of truth is one, and the followers

---

* In the second recension the name is Mandinus.

of Nature have termed it that one thing in the belly whereof is concealed the natural arcanum. This arcanum is neither seen nor known except by the Wise. He, therefore, who knows how to extract its complexion and rules equably, for him shall a nature rise forth therefrom which shall conquer all natures, and then shall that word be fulfilled which was written by the Masters, namely, that Nature rejoices in Nature, Nature overcomes Nature, and Nature contains Nature; at the same time there are not many or diverse Natures, but one having in itself its own natures and properties, by which it prevails over other things. Do you not see that the Master has begun with one and finished one? Hence has he called those unities Sulphureous Water, conquering all Nature.

The Seventy-First Dictum.

BRACUS* *saith :* How elegantly Mundus

---

* In the second recension this dictum is ascribed to Archelaus.

hath described this sulphureous water! For unless solid bodies are destroyed by a nature wanting a body, until the bodies become not-bodies, and even as a most tenuous spirit, ye cannot [attain] that most tenuous and tinge-ing soul, which is hidden in the natural belly.   And know that unless the body be withered up and so destroyed that it dies, and unless ye extract from it its soul, which is a tingeing spirit, ye are unable to tinge a body therewith.

The Seventy-Second Dictum.

PHILOSOPHUS* *saith:* The first compo-sition, that is, the body of Magnesia, is made out of several things, although they become one, and are called by one name, which the ancients have termed Albar of copper.   But when it is ruled it is called by ten names, taken from the colours which appear in the regimen of the body of this Magnesia. It is necessary, therefore, that the lead be turned into blackness; then the ten

---

* The second recension refers this dictum to Philotis.

aforesaid shall appear in the ferment of gold, with sericon,* which is a composition called by ten names. When all these things have been said, we mean nothing more by these names than Albar of copper, because it tinges every body which has entered into the composition. But composition is two-fold—one is humid, the other is dry. When they are cooked prudently they become one, and are called the good thing of several names. But when it becomes red it is called Flower of Gold, Ferment of Gold, Gold of Coral,† Gold of the Beak.‡ It is also called redundant red sulphur and red orpiment. But while it remains crude lead of copper, it is called bars and plates of metal. Behold I have re-

---

* Sericon is one of the names of Minium, according to Rulandus, but M. Berthelot explains that it was a combination of Sandyx and Sinopis.

† Later alchemical writers define Gold of Coral as the matter of the Philosophers when it has become fixed a the red stage.

‡ The significance of this phrase is, of course, perfectly inscrutable, but is there any reference to the *rostrum* or *rostellum* of the alembic ?

vealed its names when it is raw, which
also we should distinguish from the
names when it has been cooked. Let
it therefore be pondered over. It
behoves me now to exhibit to you the
quantity of the fire, and the numbers of
its days,* and the diversity of intensity
thereof in every grade, so that he who
shall possess this book may belong
unto himself,† and be freed from
poverty, so that he shall remain secure
in that middle way which is closed to
those who are deficient in this most
precious art. I have seen, therefore,
many kinds of fire. One is made out
of straw and cinder, coals and flame,
but one without flame. Experiment
shows that there are intermediate
grades between these kinds. But lead
is lead of copper, in which is the
whole arcanum. Now, concerning

---

* Greek, in common with all other alchemists, have
recognised the necessity for "a certain lapse of time and
a favourable moment." See Olympiodorus *On the Sacred
Art.*

† Compare the motto of Paracelsus : *Alterius non sit
qui suus esse potest.*

the days of the night in which will be the perfection of the most great arcanum, I will treat in its proper place in what follows. And know most assuredly that if a little gold be placed in the composition, there will result a patent and white tincture. Wherefore also a sublime gold and a patent gold is found in the treasuries of the former philosophers. Wherefore those things are unequal which they introduce into their composition. Inasmuch as the elements are commingled and are turned into lead of copper, coming out of their own former natures, they are turned into a new nature. Then they are called one nature and one genus. These things being accomplished, it is placed in a glass vessel, unless in a certain way the composition drinks the water and is altered in its colours. In every grade it is beheld, when it is coloured by a venerable redness. Although concerning this elixir we read in the sayings of the philosophers: Take gold, occurring frequently, it is only needful to do so once. Wishing, therefore, to know the certitude of the adversary, consider what Democritus* saith, how he begins speaking from bottom to top, then reversing matters he proceeds from top to bottom. For, he said : Take iron, lead, and albar† for copper, which reversing, he again says: And our copper for coins, lead for gold, gold for gold of coral, and gold of coral for gold of crocus. Again, in the second place, when he begins from the top to the bottom, he saith : Take gold, coin, copper, lead, and iron ; he shews, therefore, by his sayings that only semi-gold is taken. And without doubt gold is not changed into rust without lead and copper,

---

* Democritus at the beginning of the assembly is effectually silenced, and now seems to be quoted as an enemy at the conclusion of a symposium in which he was forbidden to participate.

† It will be well in this place to enumerate the terms, mostly of oriental origin, occurring in the *Turba* for which no explanation can at present be found. They are : Absumech, Ebmich, Corsufle, Mucra, Murtal, Geldum, Halsut, Albar, and the curious use of the Latin word Carmen.

and unless it be imbued with vinegar known by the wise, until, being cooked, it is turned into redness. This, therefore, is the redness which all the Philosophers signified, because, however they said: Take gold and it becomes gold of coral; Take gold of coral and it becomes purple gold—all these things are only names of those colours, for it behoves them that vinegar be placed in it, because these colours come from it. But by these things which the Philosophers have mentioned under various names, they have signified stronger bodies and forces. It is taken, therefore, once, that it may become rubigo and then vinegar is imposed on it. For when the said colours appear, it is necessary that each be decocted in forty days, so that it may be desiccated, the water being consumed; finally being imbued and placed in the vessel, it is cooked until its utility appear. Its first grade becomes as a citrine mucra, the second as red, the third as the dry pounded crocus of the vulgar. So is it imposed upon coin.

Conclusion.*

AGMON *saith :* I will add the following by way of a corollary. Whosoever does not liquefy and coagulate errs greatly. Therefore, make the earth black ; separate the soul and the water thereof, afterwards whiten ; so shall ye find what ye seek. I say unto you that whoso makes earth black and then dissolves with fire, till it becomes even like unto a naked sword, who also fixes the whole with consuming fire, deserves to be called happy, and shall be exalted above the circle of the world. This much concerning the revelation of our stone, is, we doubt not, enough for the Sons of the Doctrine. The strength thereof, shall never become corrupted, but the same, when it is placed in the fire, shall be increased. If you seek to dissolve, it shall be dissolved ; but if

---

* This constitutes the last Dictum in the second recension, and is omitted from the longer version.

you would coagulate, it shall be coagulated. Behold, no one is without it, and yet all do need it! There are many names given to it, and yet it is called by one only, while, if need be, it is concealed. It is also a stone and not a stone, spirit, soul, and body; it is white, volatile, concave, hairless, cold, and yet no one can apply the tongue with impunity to its surface. If you wish that it should fly, it flies; if you say that it is water, you speak the truth; if you say that it is not water, you speak falsely. Do not then be deceived by the multiplicity of names, but rest assured that it is one thing, unto which nothing alien is added. Investigate the place thereof, and add nothing that is foreign. Unless the names were multiplied, so that the vulgar might be deceived, many would deride our wisdom.

INDEX.